ADAPT OR AUTOMATE

Why AI Won't Take Your Job But Someone Who Uses It Will

Victor Lee

Copyright © 2026 by Victor Lee

Published by: Victor Lee Books
Website: victorleebooks.com

ISBN: Paperback   978 1 9194744 0 3
ISBN: Hardcover   978 1 9194744 1 0

DISCLAIMER

The information and advice presented in this book are intended for educational and informational purposes only. While the author has made every effort to ensure accuracy, AI technologies evolve rapidly. Readers should verify current capabilities and best practices for tools mentioned. The case studies in this book are based on real patterns but use composite characters and altered details to protect individual privacy. Results may vary based on individual circumstances, effort, and market conditions. This book does not constitute professional advice for your specific situation consult qualified professionals for personalized guidance.

Contact the author:
Website: victorleebooks.com
Email: hello@victorleebooks.com
Speaking inquiries: speaking@victorleebooks.com

DEDICATION

For every professional who's ever asked, *"Will AI take my job?"*
This book is your answer.

And for those who've already started adapting
Keep going. The future needs your curiosity.

ACKNOWLEDGMENTS

To every professional who's ever felt behind, overwhelmed, or unsure if they could keep up with change: this book is for you.

To the teachers, lawyers, designers, managers, entrepreneurs, and workers in every field who are navigating this transformation with courage and curiosity: you're not alone.

To the researchers and developers building AI tools that enhance rather than replace human potential: keep going.

And to you, the reader who made it to the end: thank you for investing your time in learning how to adapt, grow, and thrive.

The best is yet to come.

PRAISE FOR ADAPT OR AUTOMATE

"Victor Lee has written the book every professional needs right now. He cuts through the AI hype and fear to deliver practical wisdom that will keep you relevant for decades. I'm buying copies for my entire team."

CEO, Fortune 500 Company

"Finally, a book about AI that doesn't require a computer science degree. Accessible, actionable, and genuinely empowering. Victor bridges the gap between technical capability and human application beautifully."

Professor of Computer Science

"I went from AI-anxious to AI-confident in eight chapters. Victor's frameworks actually work, and the exercises changed how I approach my work. This is the practical guide the AI era demands."

HR Manager, Insurance Company

CONTENTS

A NOTE FROM THE AUTHOR

Welcome to the conversation.

I wrote this book because I've had the same conversation hundreds of times with professionals across industries and continents. The question is always the same: *"Will AI take my job?"*

My answer is always the same: *"No. But someone who knows how to use AI might."*

This book is that conversation, distilled into eight chapters.

Over the past decade, I've implemented AI solutions for organizations ranging from small startups to multinational enterprises, across sectors from healthcare to finance to education. I've trained thousands of professionals. I've seen what works, what doesn't, and what actually drives results.

What I've learned is this: **the technology isn't the hard part. The human side is.**

People don't fear AI because they don't understand algorithms. They fear it because they don't know where they fit in a world where machines can think, write, analyze, and create. They worry they'll become obsolete. They're afraid of being left behind.

This book is my answer to that fear. It's practical, honest, and focused on what you can do starting today to not just survive the AI era, but thrive in it.

I won't promise AI will make everything easy. I won't pretend there aren't risks. But I will show you a path forward that preserves your value, amplifies your capabilities, and keeps you in the driver's seat.

You don't need to become a technologist. You need to become adaptable.

And that's what this book will teach you.

Thank you for picking it up. Thank you for being curious enough to engage with these ideas. And thank you for being willing to adapt.

The future belongs to people like you.

Let's build it together.

Victor Lee

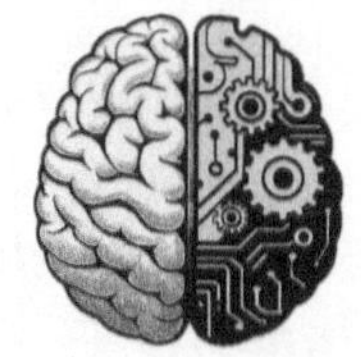

Introduction

The New Colleague

Sarah and Michael work at the same marketing agency. Same team. Same desk cluster. Same Monday morning assignment: create a competitive analysis report for a new client in the sustainable fashion industry.

Sarah opens a blank document and starts Googling. She clicks through dozens of websites, copies snippets into a Word doc, tries to organize them into themes. By Tuesday afternoon, she's got a rough draft twelve pages of bullet points and half-formed thoughts. By Wednesday, she's polishing. By Thursday morning, she emails it to her boss.

Michael takes a different approach.

He opens ChatGPT and types: *"I need to analyze the competitive landscape for sustainable fashion brands targeting millennial women in the U.S. Can you identify the top 10 brands, their unique value propositions, price points, and marketing strategies?"*

Ninety seconds later, he has a structured table. He asks follow-up questions. He challenges the AI's assumptions. He cross-references the output with recent news articles. By Monday evening, he has a polished eighteen-page report with insights Sarah hadn't even considered.

Thursday morning, when Sarah submits hers, Michael's report is already being presented to the client.

Here's what didn't happen: Michael didn't "cheat." He didn't let AI do his thinking. He used it the way a carpenter uses a power drill not to replace skill, but to amplify it.

Here's what did happen: Sarah worked hard. Michael worked smart.

And here's what will happen next: If Sarah doesn't learn what Michael learned, she won't just fall behind. She'll become invisible.

The World Has Changed. Have You?

This book is not about artificial intelligence taking your job. It's about you taking control of your future before someone else does.

The headlines scream: *"AI Will Replace Millions of Workers!" "Robots Are Coming for Your Career!"* And yes, some jobs will disappear. Some tasks will be automated. This has always been true. The printing press replaced scribes. The tractor replaced farmhands. The spreadsheet replaced rooms full of accountants with pencils.

But here's what the panic merchants won't tell you: **new tools don't destroy careers they redistribute opportunity.**

The question isn't whether AI will change your industry. It will. The question is whether you'll be the person using it, or the person replaced by someone who does.

** ** **

What This Book Will Do for You

This is not a technical manual. You won't need to learn Python or understand neural networks. This is a guidebook for the rest of us the teachers, managers, designers, salespeople, lawyers, nurses, entrepreneurs, and every other human trying to navigate a world where machines are getting smarter by the week.

You'll discover how to see AI as a co-pilot, not a competitor. The most successful people in the next decade won't be the ones who resist AI. They'll be the ones who learn to collaborate with it.

You'll learn how to use AI without losing yourself. There's a dark side to convenience. Over-reliance on AI can make us mentally lazy, passive, dependent. We'll explore how to use these tools to enhance your thinking, not replace it.

You'll understand how to future-proof your career. Jobs aren't vanishing they're evolving. You'll discover which skills are becoming more valuable (hint: the deeply human ones) and which tasks you should happily hand off to machines.

And you'll get practical steps to start today. Each chapter ends with exercises. No fluff. No theory for theory's sake. Just clear steps to begin integrating AI into your work, your learning, and your life.

** ** **

A Balanced View

I won't pretend AI is perfect. It hallucinates facts. It plagiarizes without knowing it. It can entrench bias, spread misinformation, and make us intellectually complacent if we're not careful.

But I also won't pretend you can ignore it.

Because while you're debating whether AI is good or bad, someone else someone just like you, but willing to experiment is already using it to work faster, think bigger, and deliver better results.

The future doesn't belong to AI. It belongs to people who know how to wield it.

Let's begin.

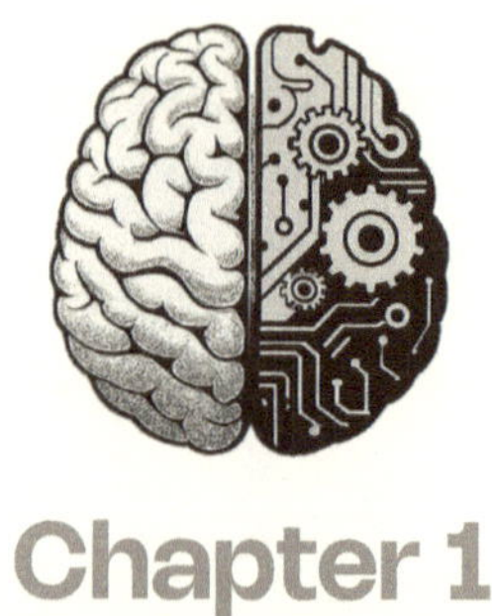

The Myth of the Job-Stealing Robot

In 1811, a group of English textile workers began smashing mechanical looms with sledgehammers. They called themselves Luddites, named after the possibly fictional Ned Ludd, who allegedly destroyed two stocking frames in a fit of rage. Their fear was simple: machines would take their jobs.

They were right. The machines did take their jobs.

But here's what happened next: the textile industry exploded. Cloth became cheaper. Demand skyrocketed. New jobs emerged machine operators, factory supervisors, logistics coordinators, designers. Within a generation, there were more people employed in textiles than before the looms arrived, just in different roles.

The Luddites weren't wrong to worry. They were wrong about what to do next.

** ** **

The Pattern Repeats

Let's fast-forward.

1900s: The tractor arrives. Farmers panic. *"We'll all starve when machines replace farmhands!"*
Result: U.S. farm employment dropped from 41% of the workforce in 1900 to 2% by 2000. But food production septupled. Meanwhile, millions moved into manufacturing, services, technology. New industries were born.

1970s: The personal computer arrives. Accountants, typists, clerks panic. *"Machines will make us obsolete!"*
Result: Routine tasks disappeared. But strategic roles exploded. The accountant who once spent weeks on ledgers now spends days on financial forecasting. The typist became the executive assistant managing complex schedules and communications.

2010s: Self-checkout kiosks arrive. Cashiers panic. *"Robots are taking our jobs!"*
Result: Some cashier jobs vanished. But grocery stores didn't shrink their staffs they redeployed workers to customer service, online order fulfillment, and inventory management.

The pattern is always the same:
Tasks disappear. Jobs evolve. Opportunity shifts to those who adapt.

** ** **

Jobs Don't Vanish. They Transform.

Here's the truth most doomsday articles miss: automation doesn't eliminate *jobs* it eliminates tasks.

A radiologist doesn't just "look at X-rays." They consult with patients, interpret results in context, collaborate with surgeons, make judgment calls when data is ambiguous. If AI can scan images for tumors faster than a human, the radiologist doesn't become obsolete they become more efficient, more strategic, more human.

A lawyer doesn't just "review contracts." They negotiate, counsel clients, navigate ethical gray areas, build trust. If AI can highlight risky clauses in seconds, the lawyer doesn't lose their job they spend more time on the work that actually matters.

A teacher doesn't just "deliver information." They inspire, mentor, adapt lessons to individual students, create safe spaces for learning. If AI can generate personalized practice problems, the teacher doesn't become redundant they become more present, more impactful.

The jobs that disappear are the ones that were only about repetitive tasks. The jobs that thrive are the ones where humans add judgment, creativity, empathy, and context.

** ** **

The Real Threat Isn't AI. It's Stagnation.

Let me be blunt: AI won't take your job.

But **someone who knows how to use AI will.**

Imagine two graphic designers. Both talented. Both experienced. Both competing for the same freelance contract.

Designer A spends eight hours sketching concepts by hand, refining them in Photoshop, tweaking color palettes.

Designer B spends two hours using AI to generate fifty concept variations, selects the strongest three, then spends six hours refining them with a level of polish and creativity that Designer A exhausted from starting from scratch can't match.

Who gets the contract?

Now multiply this across every industry. The gap between those who embrace AI and those who resist it isn't small. It's exponential.

** ** **

Why This Time Feels Different

You might be thinking: *"Okay, but AI is different. It's not just automating physical tasks it's automating thinking."*

You're right. This time is different.

AI can write. It can code. It can analyze data, generate art, diagnose diseases, compose music. It can do things we once thought were uniquely human.

Even Jeff Bezos, founder of Amazon and one of the most successful technology investors of our generation, acknowledges this fundamental shift. In a recent interview, he described AI as *"a horizontal enabling layer"* a rare type of technology that doesn't just create new industries but transforms existing ones across every sector.

"AI is real and it is going to change every industry," Bezos explained. *"The biggest impact that AI is going to have is it is going to affect every company in the world. It is going to make their quality go up and their productivity go up."* But here's what makes his perspective valuable: he doesn't just see the opportunity he sees the hype.

"Every experiment gets funded. Every company gets funded. The good ideas and the bad ideas," he observed. *"Investors have a hard time in the middle of this excitement distinguishing between the good ideas and the bad ideas."*

This is the paradox we're living through: AI is simultaneously overhyped (in terms of which companies will succeed) and underhyped (in terms of how broadly it will transform work).

Many AI startups will fail. Billions of dollars will be invested in ideas that don't work. The headlines will scream about valuations and breakthroughs that don't materialize.

But the technology itself? That's real.

LEADER PERSPECTIVE

"AI is the runtime that is going to shape all of what we do going forward in terms of the applications as well as the platform advances."

Satya Nadella, Microsoft CEO

This isn't just Bezos's view. Microsoft CEO Satya Nadella goes further: AI isn't just another tool it's becoming the fundamental infrastructure of modern work, the operating system on which everything else runs.

And Google's Sundar Pichai calls AI *"one of the most profound technologies we are working on, as important or more than fire and electricity."*
When three of the world's most successful technology leaders collectively responsible for companies worth over $5 trillion all say the same thing, it's worth paying attention.

And here's what that means for you:

The question isn't whether AI will change your industry. It will.

The question isn't whether some jobs will be automated. They will be.

The real question the only question that matters is this: **Will you be the person using AI, or the person replaced by someone who does?**

But here's the twist: **the more AI handles routine cognitive work, the more valuable non-routine human skills become.**

Let me show you what I mean.

In 2023, a study by MIT and Harvard analyzed the impact of AI on management consultants. They gave half the consultants access to GPT-4 for tasks like market analysis, customer segmentation, and idea generation.

The result?

Consultants using AI completed 12.2% more tasks and did them 25.1% faster. But here's the kicker: *the quality of their work went up by 40%* but only when they used AI as a collaborator, not a replacement.
The consultants who succeeded asked better questions, challenged the AI's assumptions, and added their own insights. The ones who blindly copied AI outputs? Their work was faster but hollow generic, surface-level, forgettable.

The lesson: **AI is a multiplier, not a substitute.** It amplifies your skills if you have them. It exposes your weaknesses if you don't.

** ** **

The New Divide

The world is splitting into two groups:

Group 1: People who see AI as a threat and avoid it. They cling to *"the old ways."* They pride themselves on doing things *"the hard way."* They fall behind, slowly at first, then all at once.
Group 2: People who see AI as a tool and master it. They experiment. They fail. They learn. They integrate AI into their workflows not to work less, but to work better. They become indispensable.
Which group do you want to be in?

The Adaptability Advantage

Charles Darwin never actually said "*survival of the fittest.*" What he said was: *"It is not the strongest of the species that survives, nor the most intelligent. It is the one most adaptable to change."*
The same is true in the workplace.

The strongest worker won't win. The smartest won't win. The one who adapts fastest will.

And here's the good news: adaptability is a skill you can learn. You don't need to become a data scientist. You don't need to understand how neural networks function. You just need to be curious, willing to experiment, and smart enough to know that the world rewards those who move forward, not those who stand still.

What's Next?

- In the chapters ahead, we'll explore:
- What AI actually is (and isn't) cutting through the hype and the fear
- The "human edge" the skills AI can't replicate and why they're more valuable than ever
- The dark side of convenience how over-reliance on AI can make us passive, lazy, and replaceable
- A practical playbook for integrating AI into your work without losing your soul
- Real stories of people who used AI to 10x their careers, and lessons from those who didn't

But first, let's get one thing straight:

This book is not about AI. It's about you.

AI is just the tool. You're the carpenter.

Let's build something remarkable.

CHAPTER 1 EXERCISE:
THE REALITY CHECK

Before moving forward, let's assess where you stand.

Take 10 minutes and answer these questions honestly:
1. **Name three tasks you do regularly at work that feel repetitive or time-consuming.**
    (Example: Drafting emails, summarizing reports, scheduling meetings)
2. **If you could save two hours a week, what would you do with that time?**
    (Example: Deep work on strategy, learning a new skill, more time with clients)
3. **On a scale of 1-10, how comfortable are you with trying new technology?**
    (Be honest. There's no wrong answer just a starting point.)
4. **What's one area where you feel like you're falling behind your peers or competitors?**
5. **If you had a "co-pilot" who could handle your least favorite tasks instantly, what would that free you up to do?**

Write down your answers. Keep them handy. By the end of this book, we'll revisit them and you'll be amazed at how much has changed.

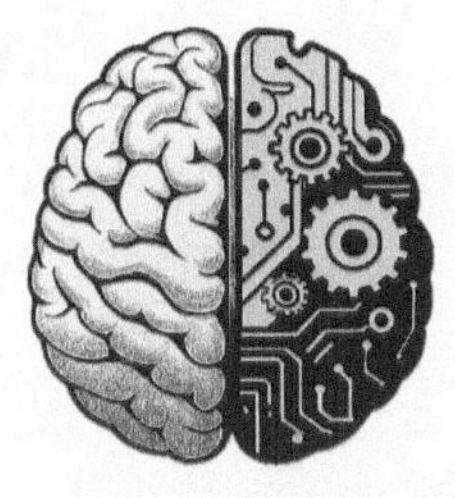

Chapter 2

Meet Your AI Toolbox

When my grandmother got her first microwave in 1985, she refused to use it for six months. It sat on the counter, gleaming and untouched, while she heated leftovers on the stove like she'd done for forty years.

"I don't trust it," she said. *"I don't understand how it works."*

My grandfather finally convinced her by making popcorn. Three minutes. Perfect. No burnt kernels. No pot to scrub.

After that, she used it every day.

She never learned the physics of electromagnetic radiation. She didn't need to. She just needed to know: *push these buttons, food gets hot, life gets easier.*

That's how you should think about AI.

You don't need to understand how a neural network processes language. You don't need to know what *"transformer architecture"* means. You just need to know which buttons to push and what each tool can do for you.

This chapter is your microwave moment.

What AI Actually Is (In 60 Seconds)

Let's cut through the jargon.

Artificial Intelligence sounds intimidating. It conjures images of sentient robots and sci-fi dystopias. But here's the reality: AI is just software that recognizes patterns and makes predictions based on massive amounts of data.

Think of it like this:

- Google Maps learns from millions of drivers to predict the fastest route.
- Netflix learns from millions of viewers to recommend shows you'll probably like.
- Your phone's autocorrect learns from billions of text messages to guess your next word.

That's AI. Pattern recognition. Prediction. Automation.

The new generation of AI the tools we're talking about in this book just does it with language, images, code, and complex reasoning instead of routes and movie preferences.

Still just patterns. Still just predictions. But powerful enough to change how you work.

⚡ KEY INSIGHT

"People understand tools and the limitations of tools more than we often give them credit for. People have found ways to make ChatGPT super useful to them and understand what not to use   it for, for the most part."

Sam Altman, OpenAI CEO

This observation from Sam Altman, CEO of OpenAI, is important. You don't need to be an AI expert to use these tools effectively. You need to be an intelligent user someone who understands both the capabilities and the constraints.

People already do this naturally. You know when to use a calculator and when to do mental math. You know when to use GPS and when your memory is good enough. You'll learn the same intuition with AI.

** ** **

The Three Types of AI You Need to Know

For practical purposes, modern AI falls into three categories. You don't need to memorize this, but understanding the basics will help you choose the right tool for the right job.

1. Generative AI (The Creator)

This is the AI that makes *stuff* text, images, music, video, code.

Examples: ChatGPT, Claude, Gemini (text); Midjourney, DALL-E (images); GitHub Copilot (code)

What it's good for:

- Writing emails, reports, proposals, blog posts
- Brainstorming ideas
- Explaining complex topics
- Drafting code
- Generating visual concepts
- Summarizing long documents

What it's bad at:

- Fact-checking itself (it confidently makes up information)
- Understanding nuance or sarcasm
- Making ethical judgments
- Replacing genuine expertise

Think of it as: A very fast, very confident intern who's read the entire internet but sometimes misremembers things.

2. Task Automation AI (The Assistant)

This is the AI that does stuff repetitive tasks you'd rather not spend time on.

Examples: Zapier, Make.com (workflow automation); Calendly (scheduling); Otter.ai (transcription); Grammarly (editing)

What it's good for:
- Scheduling meetings across time zones
- Transcribing interviews or meetings
- Moving data between apps (e.g., "When I get an email, save the attachment to Google Drive")
- Editing and proofreading
- Monitoring your inbox for specific keywords

What it's bad at:
- Handling exceptions or unusual situations
- Making judgment calls
- Understanding context beyond its specific task

Think of it as: A tireless robot assistant who follows instructions perfectly but can't improvise.

3. Analytical AI (The Analyst)

This is the AI that *finds patterns* analyzing data, spotting trends, making predictions.

Examples: Tableau (data visualization); Excel's AI features; Google Analytics; predictive text in your CRM

What it's good for:

- Analyzing sales trends
- Predicting customer behavior
- Spotting anomalies in data
- Creating visualizations
- Forecasting demand

What it's bad at:

- Understanding causation (it sees correlation, not why)
- Accounting for sudden changes or "black swan" events
- Making strategic decisions

Think of it as: A brilliant analyst who can crunch numbers faster than any human but doesn't understand the business context.

** ** **

Your Core AI Toolkit: The Big Four

You don't need twenty tools. You need four good ones. Here's where to start.

Tool 1: A Conversational AI (Your Thinking Partner)

Top choices: ChatGPT (OpenAI), Claude (Anthropic), Gemini (Google)

Cost: Free versions available; premium versions $20/month

What you'll use it for:

- Drafting and editing written content
- Brainstorming ideas
- Explaining concepts you don't understand

- Getting a second opinion on decisions
- Summarizing articles, reports, or research
- Translating languages
- Learning new skills through conversation

Real example:
Marcus, a middle school science teacher, uses ChatGPT to create differentiated lesson plans. He types: *"Create a lesson on photosynthesis for 7th graders one version for advanced students, one for students who struggle with reading."* In five minutes, he has two complete lesson plans he can refine. What used to take him two hours now takes twenty minutes.

Pro tip: The quality of what you get depends entirely on what you ask. We'll cover this in Chapter 5.

Tool 2: An Automation Platform (Your Time-Saver)

Top choices: Zapier, Make.com

Cost: Free for basic workflows; paid plans start at $20/month

What you'll use it for:

- Connecting apps so they work together automatically
- Eliminating repetitive tasks
- Building custom workflows without coding

Real example:
Jessica runs a small consulting business. Every time she gets a new client inquiry via her website, she used to manually:

- Add them to her CRM
- Send a welcome email
- Create a folder in Google Drive
- Add a task to her to-do list
-

Now? She built a Zapier workflow that does all four automatically. She saves three hours a week.

Pro tip: Start with one annoying task. Automate it. Feel the dopamine hit. Repeat.

Tool 3: A Transcription Tool (Your Note-Taker)

Top choices: Otter.ai, Fireflies.ai, Rev

Cost: Free versions available; premium around $10-20/month

What you'll use it for:

- Transcribing meetings
- Recording and organizing interviews
- Capturing brainstorming sessions
- Creating summaries and action items

Real example:
David, a project manager, uses Otter.ai in every client call. It transcribes in real-time, highlights key points, and generates action items. Instead of frantically taking notes, he's fully present in the conversation. After the call, he reviews the transcript, refines it, and sends a summary to the team. His clients constantly praise his attention to detail.

Pro tip: Always tell people you're recording. It's not just polite it's often legally required.

Tool 4: An Image Generator (Your Visual Brainstorming Partner)

Top choices: Midjourney, DALL-E, Adobe Firefly

Cost: Midjourney starts at $10/month; DALL-E has free credits; Firefly is free with Adobe subscription

What you'll use it for:

- Generating concepts for presentations
- Creating social media graphics
- Visualizing ideas
- Prototyping designs before hiring a professional

Real example:
Alicia, a startup founder, needed visuals for her pitch deck but couldn't afford a designer yet. She used Midjourney to generate concept images for her product futuristic, sleek, professional-looking

mockups. She refined them with feedback, then hired a designer to polish the final versions. The AI didn't replace the designer it got her 80% of the way there so the designer could focus on the final 20%.

Pro tip: AI-generated images are great for concepts and inspiration, but if you're publishing commercially, check the licensing terms and consider hiring a human for the final product.

** ** **

The Calculator Analogy

Here's the best way I've found to think about these tools:

In the 1970s, calculators became cheap and portable. Math teachers panicked. *"Students will forget how to do arithmetic! They'll become lazy!"*
They were half-right. Students did stop doing long division by hand. But they didn't become lazy they became *faster*. The cognitive energy they used to spend on computation, they now spent on problem-solving, logic, and real-world application.

The calculator didn't make mathematicians obsolete. It made them more powerful.

AI is the same. It handles the computational grunt work drafting, summarizing, organizing, pattern-finding so you can focus on the work that requires judgment, creativity, and wisdom.

But here's the key: **you still need to understand the math.**

A calculator won't help you if you don't know what problem you're solving. AI won't help you if you can't evaluate its output, ask the right questions, or add the human insight that turns generic content into something valuable

** ** **

What AI Can't Do (And Why That Matters)

Let's be honest about the limitations. AI is impressive, but it's not magic.

AI can't:

- Fact-check itself. It will confidently tell you things that sound true but aren't. Always verify important claims.
- Understand true context. It doesn't know your company culture, your client's personality quirks, or the unspoken dynamics in your industry.
- Feel empathy. It can mimic empathetic language, but it doesn't actually care. For anything involving human connection therapy, leadership, negotiation you're irreplaceable.
- Make ethical decisions. It has no moral compass. It will help you write a persuasive email whether your cause is noble or manipulative.

- Replace expertise. It's a tool, not a substitute for years of experience, domain knowledge, and nuanced judgment.

Think of AI like a high-powered sports car. Impressive. Fast. Powerful.

But it still needs a driver who knows where they're going.

** ** **

Getting Started: Your First AI Experiment

Theory is useless without practice. So here's your assignment.

Choose ONE tool from the list above. Just one. Trying everything at once is overwhelming.

Then do this:

Week 1: The Free Trial
Sign up. Play around. Break things. See what it can do.

Week 2: The Daily Challenge
Use it once a day for seven days. Even if it's just to write a single email or generate one idea. Build the habit.

Week 3: The Integration
Find one part of your workflow where it actually saves you time. Make it part of your routine.

By the end of three weeks, you'll know more about AI than 90% of your peers.

** ** **

The Experimenter's Mindset

Here's the secret: **the people who succeed with AI aren't the ones with the most technical knowledge. They're the ones with the most curiosity.**

They don't wait for the perfect use case. They try things. They fail. They iterate. They ask: *"What if I used this tool for that problem?"*

They treat AI like a new language. At first, they're clumsy. They make mistakes. But they keep practicing, and within weeks, they're conversational. Within months, they're fluent.

⚡ KEY INSIGHT

"This is really the time not to swim with conventional wisdom. Be playing with the technology. In fact, be introspective as to where you are in your ability to adopt new stuff and change processes, because I think that's going to be key."

Satya Nadella, Microsoft CEO

Nadella's advice is direct: Stop waiting. Stop being cautious. The cost of caution now exceeds the cost of mistakes.

You don't need to be a technologist. You just need to be willing to experiment.

A Word of Caution (That We'll Expand on Later)

Before we move on, I need to say this clearly:

Using AI is not the same as thinking.

There's a seductive trap here. AI makes things so easy that it's tempting to stop questioning, stop refining, stop thinking critically. You ask a question, it gives an answer, and you move on.
But if you do that if you outsource your thinking entirely you won't just become dependent on AI. You'll become replaceable.

The winners in the AI era will be the people who use these tools to amplify their intelligence, not replace it. We'll dive deep into this in Chapter 4. For now, just remember:

AI is a co-pilot. You're still the one flying the plane.

CHAPTER 2 EXERCISE:
YOUR FIRST AI TASK

Stop reading. Right now. Open ChatGPT, Claude, or any conversational AI.

Type this:

"I'm a [your job title] and I spend a lot of time [task you find tedious]. Can you suggest three ways AI could help me with this?"

Read the response. Pick one suggestion. Try it tomorrow.

That's it. You've just taken your first step.

Next Chapter Preview:
Chapter 3 – The Human Edge: What AI Can't Replicate (And Why You're More Valuable Than You Think)

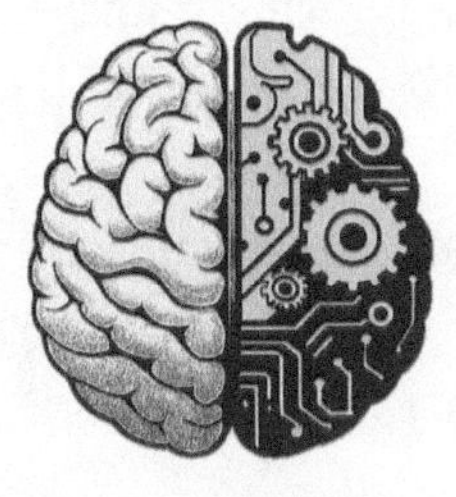

Chapter 3

The Human Edge

In 2016, Google's AlphaGo defeated Lee Sedol, one of the greatest Go players in history. It wasn't close. The AI won four games to one.

Go is a 2,500-year-old game exponentially more complex than chess. For decades, experts believed machines couldn't master it too much intuition required, too many possibilities to calculate. And yet, AlphaGo didn't just win. It played moves that human masters had never considered, strategies that defied centuries of conventional wisdom.

The chess world had already accepted this reality. Humans can't beat AI at chess anymore. We haven't been able to since 1997.

So chess died, right? Nobody plays anymore?

Wrong.

Chess has never been more popular. In 2023, Chess.com had over 150 million users. Tournament prize pools are bigger than ever. Magnus Carlsen, the world's top player, is a global celebrity.

Here's what happened: once humans stopped competing with computers, they started collaborating with them.

Chess players now use AI to analyze their games, explore new strategies, and train at levels that were impossible before. The best human players aren't the ones who memorized the most openings computers know millions of those. The best players are the ones who understand why a move works, who can improvise under pressure, who can read their opponent's psychology, who can turn a game into a story.

The machine plays perfect chess. The human plays *meaningful* chess.

That's your future with AI.

Not competition. Collaboration.

And in that collaboration, the most valuable thing you bring isn't your ability to process information faster or remember more facts. It's the things that make you *human*.

** ** **

What Humans Do Better Than Machines

Let's be precise about this. AI is remarkable at pattern recognition, data processing, and rapid output. But there are domains where humans don't just have an edge we have an insurmountable advantage.

Here are the five skills that will matter most in the age of AI.

This observation is profound. The more powerful our tools become, the more we need our humanity. The automation doesn't replace human connection it amplifies our capacity for it by freeing us from drudgery.

As Microsoft's Satya Nadella notes: *"We spend too much time consumed by the drudgery of work on tasks that zap our time, creativity, and energy. We become separated from the soul of our work."*

AI's real promise isn't replacing humans it's reconnecting us to what makes work meaningful.

Now let's look at the five human capabilities AI can't replicate.

** ** **

1. Empathy and Emotional Intelligence

AI can mimic empathy. It can say, *"I understand that must be difficult for you."* It can analyze sentiment in text and respond appropriately.

But it doesn't feel anything.

And in any situation that requires genuine human connection, that difference is everything.

Consider therapy. An AI chatbot can ask questions, provide coping strategies, even track mood patterns. Some people find AI therapy apps helpful for managing anxiety.

But when someone is in crisis grieving, traumatized, contemplating suicide they don't need an algorithm. They need a human being who can hold space for their pain, who can sense what's unspoken, who can offer the silence that says *I'm here with you.*

Consider leadership. An AI can analyze team performance metrics and suggest who should be promoted. But it can't sense the quiet frustration in someone's voice during a video call. It can't notice when a star employee is burning out before they even realize it themselves. It can't deliver tough feedback with the right balance of honesty and compassion.

Consider sales. AI can personalize an email based on someone's browsing history. But it can't read the room in a negotiation. It can't pivot when it senses the client is hesitant for reasons they haven't voiced. It can't build the kind of trust that turns a transaction into a long-term relationship.

Empathy is pattern recognition plus *care.* AI has the first. Only humans have both.

The opportunity: As AI handles more transactional interactions, the premium on *genuine* human connection will skyrocket. The customer service rep who makes someone feel heard. The manager who truly understands their team. The salesperson who listens more than they pitch. These people will become indispensable.

** ** **

2. Judgment in Ambiguous Situations

AI excels in structured environments. Give it clear rules and defined goals, and it's unstoppable.

But the real world is messy. Full of gray areas. Full of situations where the *"right"* answer depends on context, values, competing priorities, and factors that can't be quantified.

Example: The hospital dilemma

Imagine you're an emergency room doctor. Two patients arrive simultaneously. One is a 28-year-old mother of three with a severe allergic reaction. The other is a 74-year-old man having a heart attack.

Both need immediate attention. You have one team.

Who do you treat first?

An AI could process survival probabilities, expected years of life saved, statistical outcomes. It could give you a recommendation based on data.

But it can't tell you how to weigh the value of a young mother's life against an elderly man's. It can't factor in that the older man is a beloved community leader who mentors at-risk youth. It can't account for the trauma the medical team will carry if they make the *"wrong"* choice.

This isn't a math problem. It's a moral problem. And humans have spent millennia developing frameworks for navigating these impossible situations not perfectly, but thoughtfully.

The opportunity: In law, medicine, business ethics, policy, and countless other fields, the ability to navigate ambiguity with wisdom not just data will be the defining skill. AI can inform your decision. Only you can make it.

** ** **

3. Creativity That Breaks Patterns

Wait doesn't AI create art? Doesn't it write novels and compose music?

Yes. And it's impressive. But there's a crucial difference between *recombination* and *innovation.*

AI generates by recognizing patterns in existing data. It creates new outputs by mixing and matching what already exists. It's phenomenally good at this. It can write a poem in the style of Emily Dickinson, paint like Van Gogh, compose a symphony that sounds like Mozart.

But it can't do what those artists did: **create something the world has never seen.**

Consider the Beatles. In 1964, they merged rock and roll with Indian classical music on *"Norwegian Wood."* Nobody had done that before. There was no pattern to recognize. It was a leap of imagination that came from curiosity, cultural exposure, and the willingness to break rules.

Consider Pixar. When they made *Toy Story*, they weren't following a template. They invented computer-animated feature films. They took enormous risks. They failed repeatedly. They persisted because they believed in something that didn't exist yet.

Consider Steve Jobs. When he introduced the iPhone, he didn't survey customers about what they wanted in a phone they would've said *"a better keyboard."* He imagined something radically different and convinced the world they needed it.

This kind of creativity **the kind that defines new categories rather than optimizing existing ones** requires intuition, risk-taking, and the ability to see connections across unrelated domains.

AI can help you brainstorm. It can generate 100 variations on an idea. But the leap from *"good"* to *"revolutionary"*? That's still human territory.

The opportunity: The future belongs to people who can use AI to handle the mundane creative work (drafting, iterating, refining) so they can focus on the *visionary* creative work the ideas that don't come from data, but from imagination.

** ** **

4. Cross-Domain Synthesis

AI is narrow. Even the most advanced models are specialists. An AI trained on medical data is brilliant at diagnosing diseases but useless at designing buildings.

Humans, on the other hand, are **connection machines.** We pull insights from one domain and apply them to another. We see patterns across disciplines. We synthesize.

Example: Velcro

In 1941, Swiss engineer George de Mestral went hiking. When he got home, he noticed burrs stuck to his dog's fur. Instead of just pulling them off, he examined them under a microscope. He saw tiny hooks that caught on loops in the fabric.

That observation from nature inspired Velcro. He synthesized biology and engineering.

AI could never make that leap. It doesn't go hiking. It doesn't have a dog. It doesn't look at burrs and think, *"What if we made fasteners like this?"*

Example: The iPod

Steve Jobs didn't invent the MP3 player. He combined existing technologies hard drives, lithium batteries, software, design in a way nobody else had thought to. He pulled from tech, music industry insights, and consumer behavior to create something new.

The opportunity: The more specialized AI becomes, the more valuable *generalists* become people who can connect ideas across industries, who read widely, who bring unconventional perspectives to conventional problems.

Want to be irreplaceable? Be the person in the room who says, *"You know what solved this problem in a completely different field? Let me tell you..."*

** ** **

5. Building Trust and Long-Term Relationships

AI can send personalized emails at scale. It can remember your birthday. It can tailor its communication style to match yours.

But trust isn't built through personalization. It's built through *consistency over time, vulnerability, and shared experience.*

Example: The mentor

Think about the best mentor you've ever had. What made them valuable?

Probably not their ability to give you information you could Google most of what they taught you. What made them irreplaceable was:

- They believed in you when you doubted yourself
- They shared their failures, not just their successes
- They gave you honest feedback, even when it was hard to hear
- They opened doors for you because they genuinely wanted you to succeed

An AI can simulate mentorship. It can answer questions, provide encouragement, suggest career moves.

But it can't *care* about your success. It can't feel pride when you achieve something. It can't take a personal risk to advocate for you.

Example: The family doctor

In small towns, the family doctor isn't just a medical provider they're a trusted advisor who knows your history, your family dynamics, your fears. When they recommend a treatment, you trust them not just because of their medical knowledge, but because they've *been there* through your life's ups and downs.

That's irreplaceable.

The opportunity: In an age of automation, the businesses that thrive will be the ones that invest in *relationships,* not just transactions. The financial advisor who checks in when the market crashes. The teacher who remembers every student's name five years later. The boss who fights for their team's raises.

These people don't just provide a service. They become part of people's lives.

** ** **

The Paradox of AI: It Makes Soft Skills Hard Currency

Here's the twist nobody saw coming:

We thought AI would replace *"soft skills"* and reward technical skills. We thought engineers and data scientists would rule the world.

But the opposite is happening.
As AI handles the technical work, the *"soft skills"* become the *only* skills that matter.

Communication. Persuasion. Collaboration. Leadership. Emotional intelligence. Adaptability.

These used to be called *"soft"* because they were harder to measure than technical proficiency. Now they're the **hardest skills to automate** and therefore the most valuable.

The irony is perfect. The more advanced AI becomes, the more we need to be deeply, authentically, *irreplaceably* human.

** ** **

The Question You Should Be Asking

Not: *"Will AI take my job?"*

But: *"Which parts of my job are the most human?"*

Those are the parts to double down on. Those are the parts that will make you indispensable.

Let's try an exercise.

Take your job and divide your tasks into two columns:

Column A: Tasks a well-trained AI could do
(Data entry, scheduling, research, drafting standard documents, summarizing reports)

Column B: Tasks that require your humanity
(Building client relationships, mentoring team members, making ethical calls, creative strategy, handling sensitive conversations)

Now ask yourself: **How much of your time is currently spent in Column A vs. Column B?**

If you're spending 80% of your time on Column A tasks, you're vulnerable. Not because AI will replace you tomorrow, but because **someone who spends 20% on Column A and 80% on Column B will outperform you.**

The goal isn't to avoid AI. It's to use AI to automate Column A so you can dominate Column B.

**** ** ****

The New Professional

Let me paint you a picture of what the most successful professional looks like in 2030.

Meet Priya.

She's a marketing director at a mid-sized company. Every morning, she reviews reports that AI generated overnight campaign performance, competitor analysis, trend forecasts. She spends 15 minutes on this. It used to take her three hours.

Then she spends two hours in meetings. Not presenting data the team already has that. She's reading the room. She's sensing who's frustrated, who's energized, who needs support. She's building consensus on a bold creative direction that the data suggests is risky but her intuition says will resonate.

She spends an hour mentoring a junior team member, not teaching them *what* to do (AI can do that), but helping them think critically about *why* a campaign worked and building their confidence to take creative risks.

She spends another hour on a client call. The AI already drafted the proposal. She's there to build trust, to listen to what the client isn't saying, to adapt the strategy based on subtle cues in the conversation.

At the end of the day, she asks AI to summarize the meeting notes, draft follow-up emails, and create three variations of the campaign concept to review tomorrow.

She's working the same hours as she did five years ago. But she's 3x more effective because she's spending her time on the work that *only she* can do.

That's not science fiction. That's happening right now.

** ** **

Your Competitive Advantage Isn't Knowledge Anymore

For most of human history, knowing more gave you an edge. The person who'd read the most books, memorized the most facts, accumulated the most expertise they won.

AI has shattered that equation.

Now, **knowing things is table stakes. Everyone has access to the same information.** What matters is what you do with it.

Your competitive advantage is:

- **Asking better questions** than the AI would ask itself
- **Connecting ideas** from different domains
- **Making judgment calls** when the data is ambiguous
- **Building relationships** that turn one-time clients into lifelong advocates
- **Leading teams** through uncertainty with empathy and clarity

These are the skills that separate good from great. And none of them can be automated.

** ** **

The Most Important Question

Here's what I want you to sit with:
What makes you human isn't what you know. It's how you connect, how you care, how you create, and how you choose.

AI can process. Only you can *prioritize.*
AI can suggest. Only you can *decide.*

AI can draft. Only you can *refine* with taste and wisdom.
The question isn't whether AI will change your work. It will.

The question is: **will you use it to become more human, or less?**

CHAPTER 3 EXERCISE:
FIND YOUR IRREPLACEABLE WORK

This week, do this:

Step 1: At the end of each workday, write down the 3-5 tasks you spent the most time on.

Step 2: Next to each task, mark whether it required your humanity (judgment, empathy, creativity, relationships) or whether it was primarily mechanical (data processing, formatting, research, scheduling).

Step 3: At the end of the week, calculate your ratio. How much of your time is spent being irreplaceably human vs. doing work a machine could do?

Step 4: Pick ONE mechanical task. Next week, use AI to automate or accelerate it. Use the time saved to invest in the human work the conversation you've been putting off, the creative project that needs deeper thought, the relationship that needs nurturing.

Step 5: Notice how it feels. Not just the time saved, but the shift in *what you're spending your energy on.*

That shift? That's your future.

Next Chapter Preview:
Chapter 4 – The Lazy Brain Trap: How AI Can Make You Smarter Or Dumber

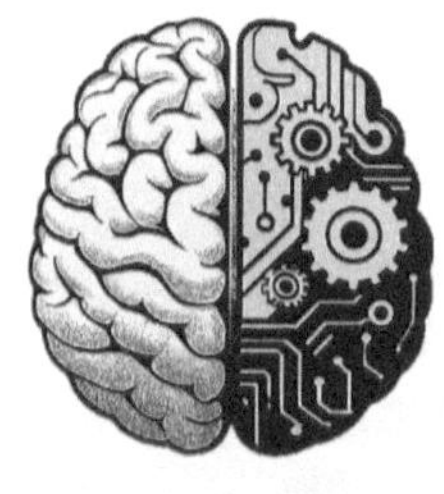

Chapter 4

The Lazy Brain Trap

In 2008, a team of neuroscientists at University College London published a startling study.

They'd been tracking London taxi drivers the famous *"black cab"* drivers who spend years memorizing every street, alley, and shortcut in one of the world's most complex cities. To get their license, they must pass *"The Knowledge,"* an grueling test that takes 3-4 years of study.

Brain scans showed something remarkable: these drivers had significantly larger hippocampi (the brain region responsible for spatial memory) than average Londoners. Their brains had physically changed in response to the mental demands of navigation.

Then GPS became ubiquitous.

In 2020, the same research team did a follow-up study. They found that newer taxi drivers those who'd trained using GPS rather than pure memorization showed no such brain development. Their hippocampi were normal-sized.

And among the veteran drivers who'd switched to GPS? Their hippocampi had *shrunk.*

The technology hadn't just changed how they navigated. It had changed their brains.

Here's the uncomfortable truth we need to talk about:

AI can make you smarter, faster, and more productive. Or it can make you cognitively lazy, intellectually passive, and ultimately replaceable.
The difference isn't the technology. It's how you use it.

** ** **

The Seduction of Convenience

Let me tell you about two students. Both college juniors. Both taking the same marketing class. Both assigned to write a 10-page analysis of a failed product launch.

Student A: Emma

Emma opens ChatGPT. Types: *"Write a 10-page analysis of why Google Glass failed, including market analysis, competitor comparison, and lessons learned."*

The AI produces a polished essay in 90 seconds. Emma skims it. Looks good. She copies it into a document, changes a few words to avoid plagiarism detection, and submits it.

Total time invested: 20 minutes.

Student B: James

James opens ChatGPT. Types: *"What were the main reasons Google Glass failed?"*

The AI lists five factors. James reads them, then asks: *"Can you explain the privacy concerns in more detail?"*

The AI elaborates. James takes notes. Then he asks: *"What other products failed for similar reasons?"*
The AI mentions Segway and Amazon Fire Phone. James now has a pattern to explore.

He spends the next two hours researching, reading original articles, watching interviews with Google executives, comparing the AI's claims against real sources. He uses the AI to help him organize his thoughts, test his arguments, and refine his writing.

The AI drafts sections. James rewrites them in his own voice, adding insights the AI missed.

Total time invested: four hours.

Three months later, they're both in job interviews.

The interviewer asks Emma: *"Tell me about a time you analyzed why a product failed."*

Emma freezes. She remembers the assignment. She remembers turning it in. But she can't remember anything *in* the essay. It never entered her brain it went from the AI directly to the professor.

She mumbles something generic about *"market fit"* and *"timing."*

James, meanwhile, lights up. He talks about the privacy backlash against Google Glass, draws parallels to current tech products, discusses how consumer sentiment has shifted. He references specific incidents, quotes executives, shows he understands *why* things failed, not just *that* they failed.

Who gets the job?

** ** **

Use It or Lose It: The Cognitive Decline Risk

Your brain is not a hard drive. It's a muscle.

And like any muscle, it atrophies when you stop using it.

This isn't speculation. It's neuroscience.

The *"Google Effect"* (also called *"digital amnesia"*) was documented in 2011 by psychologist Betsy Sparrow at Columbia University. She found that when people know information is easily accessible online, they don't bother remembering it. Instead, they remember *where* to find it.

Sounds efficient, right? Outsource memory to the internet, free up mental space for higher-level thinking.

Except that's not what happened.

Further research showed that people weren't using that *"freed up"* mental space for deeper thinking. They were just consuming more shallow information. They'd become skilled at *finding answers*, but less skilled at *understanding* them.

Now multiply that effect by 1000 with AI.
It's not just facts we can outsource anymore. It's thinking, writing, problem-solving, creativity. And the easier it becomes, the more tempting it is to stop doing the hard cognitive work.

Here's the danger:

- **AI writes your emails** → you forget how to communicate persuasively
- **AI summarizes articles** → you lose the ability to identify key ideas yourself
- **AI solves problems** → you stop developing problem-solving skills
- **AI generates ideas** → your creative muscles atrophy
- **AI writes code** → you stop understanding what the code actually does

You don't notice the decline day by day. But over months and years? You wake up one day and realize you can't do the work without the AI anymore.

And that's when you become replaceable.

The Autopilot Effect: When Convenience Becomes Dependency

Have you ever driven somewhere on autopilot and not remembered the journey? You arrived safely, but you have no memory of the last 20 minutes?

That's your brain optimizing for efficiency. It recognizes a pattern (familiar route, no surprises) and disengages active attention.

The same thing happens with AI.

Use it often enough, and you stop thinking about what you're doing. You just input a prompt, accept the output, move on.

You're on cognitive autopilot.

Real example: The junior developer

A software company hired a promising junior developer. Six months in, his productivity was impressive tickets closed twice as fast as his peers.

But his senior colleagues noticed something odd: he couldn't explain how his code worked. When bugs appeared, he couldn't debug them. He'd just ask the AI to fix it, copy the new code, and move on.

He wasn't learning. He was dependent.

When the company implemented stricter AI usage policies (requiring developers to explain their code in reviews), his productivity plummeted. He couldn't function without the crutch.

He wasn't fired, but he wasn't promoted either. He'd plateaued at junior level because he'd outsourced the struggle that builds expertise.

The pattern:

1. AI makes task easier
2. You stop engaging deeply with the task
3. Your skills don't develop
4. You become dependent on AI
5. When AI makes an error (and it will), you can't catch it
6. When AI isn't available, you can't function

This isn't a future risk. It's happening now.

The Two Types of AI Users: Pilots vs. Passengers

Here's the framework that matters:

Passengers let AI drive. They input a task, accept the output, and move on. They save time, but they don't learn. They don't improve. They don't think critically about what the AI produces.

Pilots use AI as a co-pilot. They stay engaged. They question outputs. They iterate. They add their own judgment. They use AI to go faster and further, but they're always in control.

CRITICAL WARNING

"AI is going to eliminate a lot of current jobs, and there will be classes of jobs that totally   go away. AI is also going to change the way a   lot of current jobs function, and it's going to   create entirely new jobs."

Sam Altman, OpenAI CEO

Notice what Altman is saying: jobs that "*totally go away*" are typically those that involve only repetitive tasks with no judgment, creativity, or human connection. If your job can be reduced to a predictable algorithm, you're vulnerable. If it requires the human skills we discussed in Chapter 3, you're valuable.

The difference between pilots and passengers determines which category you fall into.

Let me show you the difference in practice.

Example 1: Writing a Report

Passenger approach:

- Prompt: *"Write a 5-page report on renewable energy trends"*
- Copy output
- Submit

Pilot approach:

- Prompt: *"What are the top 5 renewable energy trends in 2025?"*
- Read output, identify gaps
- Prompt: *"You mentioned solar storage innovations can you give specific examples with companies and technologies?"*
- Cross-check facts against recent news
- Prompt: *"Draft an introduction that hooks readers with a surprising statistic"*
- Rewrite it in own voice
- Prompt: *"What's the strongest counterargument to renewable energy adoption?"*
- Add nuanced section addressing concerns
- Final product: AI-assisted, but thoroughly human

Example 2: Solving a Business Problem

Passenger approach:

- Prompt: "*How do we increase customer retention?*"
- Copy the 10 suggestions AI provides
- Present to team

Pilot approach:

- Prompt: "*What factors typically influence customer retention in SaaS companies?*"
- Evaluate which factors apply to our *specific* business
- Prompt: "*Our churn happens mostly at the 3-month mark what does that suggest?*"
- Use AI's framework to analyze internal data
- Prompt: "*Critique this retention strategy I'm considering...*"
- Test AI's logic, push back on weak points
- Final product: Strategy informed by AI, but tailored to specific context

The difference?

Passengers treat AI like a vending machine: insert query, receive answer, consume.

Pilots treat AI like a sparring partner: propose, challenge, refine, synthesize.

Passengers save time but stay stagnant.
Pilots invest time and compound their skills.

The Four Cognitive Traps (And How to Avoid Them)

Let's get specific about where things go wrong and how to protect yourself.

Trap 1: The Accuracy Illusion

AI sounds confident even when it's wrong. It doesn't say *"I think"* or *"maybe."* It states things as facts.

This creates a dangerous illusion: we assume polished language = accurate information.

The trap: You stop fact-checking because the output sounds authoritative.

The antidote:
- Always verify critical facts, especially numbers, dates, quotes, or technical claims
- Ask yourself: *"How would I verify this if AI didn't exist?"*
- Use AI to find sources, but always check the source yourself
- When AI cites a study, look up the actual study AI often misrepresents findings

Real example: A marketing manager asked AI to analyze competitor pricing. The AI confidently listed prices for five competitors. Three were accurate. Two were completely made up. The manager nearly presented false data to executives because it looked so professional.

Trap 2: The Depth Sacrifice

AI gives you breadth fast. But breadth isn't depth.

It can summarize a 50-page report in 30 seconds. But that summary misses nuance, context, and the subtle arguments that separate good thinking from great thinking.

The trap: You consume summaries instead of engaging with primary material. You become intellectually shallow.

The antidote:

- Use AI for triage, not replacement. Let it tell you which sources are worth your deep attention
- For anything important, read the original source yourself
- Ask AI to summarize, then read the original and notice what the summary *missed*
- Treat AI summaries as previews, not substitutes

Mental model: AI is like movie trailers. They tell you what the movie is about, but they're not the same as watching the movie.

Trap 3: The Creativity Shortcut

AI can generate ideas fast. 100 brainstorm ideas in 10 seconds.
But quantity isn't quality. And more importantly, **the struggle to generate ideas is where creativity develops.**

When you bypass that struggle, you don't build the creative muscle.

The trap: You stop thinking for yourself. You treat AI's first output as *"good enough."*

The antidote:

- Start with your own ideas first. Brainstorm for 10 minutes before asking AI
- Use AI to expand your thinking, not replace it
- When AI gives you ideas, push back: "What's the opposite approach?" "What's the riskiest version?" "What would make this more original?"
- Pick AI's weakest idea and challenge yourself to make it work this builds creative problem-solving

The principle: AI should be a sparring partner, not a shortcut past the thinking.

Trap 4: The Skill Erosion

Every time AI does something for you, you're forgoing an opportunity to practice that skill.

This is fine for skills that don't matter to your career. But it's career suicide for core skills.

The trap: You outsource so much that your skills atrophy. When AI makes an error, you can't catch it. When AI isn't available, you can't function.

The antidote:

- Identify your core skills the ones that define your professional value
- For core skills: use AI to assist, not replace. Let it draft, but you must rewrite. Let it suggest, but you must decide
- For peripheral skills: automate freely
- Deliberately practice core skills without AI regularly like an athlete training without equipment

Example: If you're a writer, your core skill is crafting compelling prose. Use AI to research, organize, and draft but the final writing must be yours. Don't let AI write your voice away.

If you're a data analyst, your core skill is interpreting patterns and making recommendations. Use AI to clean data and generate visualizations but the insights must come from you.

** ** **

The Goldilocks Principle: Not Too Much, Not Too Little

So what's the right amount of AI to use?

The answer is frustratingly nuanced: **it depends on whether you're building skills or deploying them.**

When you're learning (new role, new skill, new domain):

→ Use AI *less*. You need the struggle. You need to make mistakes. You need to build mental models.
When you're performing (established skill, routine task, high-volume work):
→ Use AI *more*. You've already built the skill. Now leverage AI to scale it.

Think of it like training wheels on a bike.

When you're learning to ride, training wheels help you get started. But you need to remove them to actually develop balance.

AI is your training wheels. Use them when you need support. Remove them when you need growth.

** ** **

The Pilot's Checklist: 10 Rules for Staying Sharp

Here's your practical framework for using AI without losing yourself:

1. Never accept AI's first output as final. Always refine, question, personalize.

2. For important work, fact-check everything. Trust, but verify.

3. Use AI to draft, but you must edit. Your voice, your judgment, your responsibility.

4. Start with your own thinking first. Then use AI to challenge and expand it.

5. Read original sources, not just summaries. Depth matters more than speed.

6. Practice core skills regularly without AI. Like working out without performance enhancers.

7. When AI makes an error, understand why. This builds your ability to catch future errors.

8. Explain AI's output in your own words. If you can't, you don't understand it.

9. Use AI for tasks you've already mastered. Automate competence, not learning.
10. Ask yourself weekly: *"Am I using AI as a crutch or a catalyst?"* Be honest.

The Ultimate Test: The Blackout Question

Here's how you know if you're using AI well:

Imagine AI disappeared tomorrow. Could you still do your job at a high level?

If the answer is yes you'd be slower, but still competent you're using it right.

If the answer is no you'd be lost you've become dependent.
The goal isn't to avoid AI. It's to use AI in a way that makes you more capable, not less.

** ** **

Why This Matters More Than You Think

Let's zoom out for a moment.
We're not just talking about productivity hacks here. We're talking about your cognitive autonomy your ability to think independently, solve problems creatively, and add unique value.

In a world where everyone has access to the same AI, **your differentiation comes from what you do with it.**

Two people use the same AI tool. One becomes more insightful, more creative, more valuable. The other becomes passive, generic, replaceable.

The tool is the same. The outcome is radically different.

The determining factor? How engaged your brain stays in the process.

** ** **

The Hope: AI as a Cognitive Gym

Here's the reframe that changes everything:

What if you used AI not to avoid thinking, but to *think harder?*

- Use it to challenge your ideas
- Use it to expose you to perspectives you wouldn't have considered
- Use it to test your arguments
- Use it to learn faster by asking better questions

This is AI as a cognitive gym, not a cognitive crutch.

Example:

Instead of: *"Write an argument for renewable energy"*

Try: *"I believe renewable energy is the future. Now argue against my position as strongly as possible."*

Then strengthen your argument by addressing those counterpoints.
You're not outsourcing thinking. You're upgrading your thinking by pressure-testing it.

The Choice Is Yours

AI is like fire.

You can use it to cook food and stay warm. Or you can burn your house down.

The fire doesn't choose. You do.
Every time you use AI, you're making a choice:

- Pilot or passenger?
- Thinking partner or thinking replacement?
- Cognitive growth or cognitive decline?

The technology won't make that choice for you.

Only you can.

**CHAPTER 4 EXERCISE:
THE DEPENDENCY AUDIT**
This week, run an experiment.

Day 1-3: Use AI normally
Track how often you use it and for what.

Day 4-6: Go AI-free
Do the same tasks without any AI assistance.

Day 7: Reflect
Answer these questions:

1. What tasks were impossible without AI? (These
    might be legitimate use cases)
2. What tasks were just slower without AI? (Good
    candidates for AI assistance)
3. What tasks revealed skills you've let atrophy? (Red
    flags)
4. Where did you miss AI most for speed, or because
    you genuinely couldn't do the task anymore? (This
    reveals dependency)
5. On a scale of 1-10, how confident are you in your
    core professional skills independent of AI?

If you scored below 7 on question 5, it's time to rebuild.

The rest of this book will show you how.

Next Chapter Preview:
*Chapter 5 – The Practical Playbook: How to Actually
Learn AI (Without Becoming Dependent On It)*

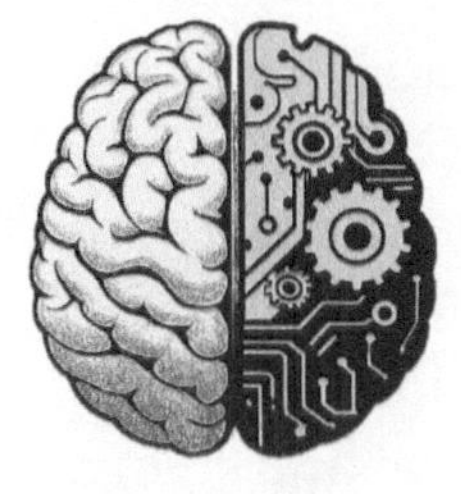

Chapter 5

The Practical Playbook

In 1964, a psychologist named Benjamin Bloom published a study that would change education forever.

He discovered that students who received one-on-one tutoring performed two standard deviations better than students in traditional classrooms. This became known as the *"2 Sigma Problem"* how do you give every student the benefit of personalized instruction?

For 60 years, we couldn't solve it. One-on-one tutoring doesn't scale. There aren't enough tutors. It's too expensive.

Until now.

AI isn't just a tool for doing work faster. It's a personal tutor available 24/7, in your pocket, for the cost of a streaming subscription.

But like any tutor, it's only as good as the questions you ask.

This chapter is your guide to asking better questions and using AI not just to work, but to *learn*.

The Core Principle: Prompt Like a Boss, Not a Beginner

Most people use AI like a search engine.

They type: *"Marketing ideas"*
AI responds with generic suggestions.
They shrug and move on.

This is like walking into a five-star restaurant and saying, *"Food, please."* You'll get something, but not what the chef is capable of creating.

The secret to getting exceptional output from AI isn't understanding how it works. It's understanding how to *communicate* what you want.

Good prompts are:

- **Specific** (not vague)
- **Contextual** (include relevant details)
- **Role-based** (tell AI what perspective to take)
- **Constrained** (give parameters and formats)
- **Iterative** (built on previous responses)

Let me show you.

The Prompt Framework: From Weak to Powerful

Level 1: The Beginner (Vague)

"Write a marketing email."

What you get: Generic, forgettable copy that sounds like every other marketing email.

Level 2: The Intermediate (Specific)

"Write a marketing email for a new fitness app targeting busy professionals."

What you get: Better. At least it has a direction.

Level 3: The Advanced (Contextual + Role-based)

"You're a marketing copywriter known for conversational, benefit-driven emails. Write a 150-word email announcing our new fitness app to busy professionals aged 30-45 who've tried fitness apps before but quit. Focus on the unique feature: 15-minute workouts that adapt to your schedule. Tone: encouraging but not preachy. Include a clear call-to-action."

What you get: Targeted, purposeful copy that actually sounds like something you'd send.

Level 4: The Expert (Iterative + Constrained)

Start with Level 3, then:

"Now rewrite it with a subject line that uses curiosity rather than benefit."
"Give me three variations one focused on time-saving, one on results, one on convenience."

"The opening line feels weak. Give me five alternative opening lines that hook the reader immediately."

"This sounds too corporate. Make it sound like a friend recommending an app, not a company selling one."
What you get: Polished, refined copy that's actually usable and you learned something about what makes copy work.

The pattern:

Bad prompts = vague requests + accepting first output
Good prompts = specific context + iterative refinement

The Six-Step AI Learning Loop

Here's the process that turns AI from a shortcut into a skill-builder.

Step 1: Attempt It Yourself First

Before touching AI, spend 10 minutes thinking through the problem yourself.
- If it's writing: Draft a rough outline
- If it's problem-solving: Brainstorm 3-5 approaches
- If it's creative: Generate a few ideas
- If it's analysis: Form a hypothesis

Why this matters: This primes your brain. When AI responds, you'll evaluate it critically rather than passively accepting it.

Step 2: Give AI Rich Context

Don't just ask a question. Set the stage.

Weak: *"How do I improve team productivity?"*

Strong: *"I manage a team of 8 remote software developers. Our main productivity issue is fragmented communication people ask the same questions repeatedly, decisions get lost in Slack threads, and new team members take weeks to get up to speed. What are three strategies to improve knowledge management and reduce communication overhead?"*

The more context you provide, the more tailored the response.

Step 3: Assign AI a Role

Want better advice? Tell AI who to be.

- *"You're a seasoned CFO advising a startup..."*
- *"You're a high school teacher with 20 years of experience..."*
- *"You're a UX designer critiquing this interface..."*
- *"You're a skeptical investor poking holes in this business plan..."*

Roles give AI a lens through which to filter its response.

Step 4: Challenge the Output

This is where most people stop. Don't.

After AI responds, push back:

- *"What are the weaknesses in this approach?"*
- *"What would a critic say about this?"*
- *"What am I not considering?"*
- *"Play devil's advocate argue against this strategy."*
- *"What would happen if the opposite were true?"*

You're not just getting answers. You're stress-testing your thinking.

Step 5: Synthesize in Your Own Words

After the conversation, close the AI and write a summary yourself.

Don't copy-paste AI's words. Translate them.

This forces comprehension. If you can't explain it in your own words, you didn't really learn i

Step 6: Apply and Reflect

Take action based on what you learned. Then reflect:

- What worked?
- What didn't?
- What would you ask differently next time?
- What surprised you?

This is the compounding step. Each cycle makes you better at using AI and better at the underlying skill.

** ** **

Real-World Applications: AI for Your Actual Job

Let's get specific. Here's how different professionals can use AI as a learning accelerator.

For Teachers: AI as Curriculum Designer

The old way:
Spend hours creating lesson plans, worksheets, and assessments from scratch.

The AI way:

Prompt: *"I'm teaching 9th grade biology. Tomorrow's lesson is on cellular respiration. Create a 50-minute lesson plan that includes: a 10-minute hook using a real-world example, a 25-minute explanation with visuals I can describe verbally, and a 15-minute hands-on activity. Make sure it addresses common misconceptions students have about this topic."*
AI generates a full lesson plan.

But don't stop there. Level up:
"What analogies work best for explaining the electron transport chain to visual learners?"

"Create five quiz questions two easy, two medium, one challenging with answers and explanations."

"A student just asked, 'Why do we even need to breathe?' Give me a simple but scientifically accurate answer that a 14-year-old will find interesting."

What you're learning: How to structure lessons, explain complex concepts simply, anticipate student questions.

The pilot move: Use AI's lesson plan as a foundation, but customize it based on your students' needs and your teaching style.

For Lawyers: AI as Research Assistant

The old way:
Spend billable hours combing through case law and legal databases.

The AI way:

Prompt: *"I'm preparing a defense for a client accused of breach of contract. The plaintiff claims my client failed to deliver services on time, but the contract includes a force majeure clause. Find me precedents where force majeure clauses were successfully invoked in service contracts during economic downturns."*
AI provides cases and summaries.

Level up:

"What are the strongest counterarguments the opposing counsel might use?"
"Draft a paragraph arguing why the force majeure clause applies in this case, citing the precedents you found."
"Now critique that paragraph as if you were the opposing lawyer."

What you're learning: Legal reasoning, argumentation strategies, anticipating opposition.

The pilot move: Verify every case citation (AI sometimes invents cases), read the original rulings, and add your legal judgment to the arguments.

For Entrepreneurs: AI as Strategy Partner

The old way:
Guesswork, trial and error, expensive consultants.

The AI way:

Prompt: *"I'm launching a meal prep service targeting young professionals in Austin, Texas. My competitors are Factor and HelloFresh. My differentiation is locally-sourced ingredients and same-day delivery. What are the three biggest risks to this business model, and how should I mitigate them?"*

AI identifies risks: logistics complexity, thin margins, customer acquisition cost.
Level up:

"How much should I budget for customer acquisition in the first six months?"

"What metrics should I track weekly to know if the business is viable?"
"Give me a breakdown of operational costs for delivering 100 meals per day."

"What would a seasoned food industry investor want to see in my pitch deck?"

What you're learning: Business fundamentals, financial planning, risk assessment.

The pilot move: Cross-reference AI's numbers with real data (industry reports, competitor pricing, actual vendor quotes). Use AI as a starting point, not the final word.

For Designers: AI as Creative Sparring Partner

The old way:
Stare at blank canvas. Hope inspiration strikes.

The AI way:

Prompt: *"I'm designing a logo for an eco-friendly sneaker brand targeting Gen Z. The brand values are sustainability, style, and authenticity. Give me 10 concept directions some literal, some abstract."*

AI suggests concepts: leaf motifs, footprint designs, minimalist geometric shapes, vintage athletic aesthetics, etc.

Level up:

"Take the 'footprint that transforms into a tree' concept. What are three visual ways to execute that?"
"What colors would reinforce the eco-friendly message without feeling cliché?"

"Critique this concept: Would it work at small sizes? Would it stand out against competitors?"

"What design trends should I avoid so this doesn't feel dated in two years?"

What you're learning: Conceptual thinking, design principles, trend awareness.

The pilot move: Use AI's concepts as inspiration, not final designs. Sketch your interpretations. Add your unique style. The AI generates ideas; you create art.

For Managers: AI as Leadership Coach

The old way:
React to problems as they arise. Learn through trial and error.

The AI way:

Prompt: *"I manage a team of 10. One of my best performers has been missing deadlines and seems disengaged in meetings. I suspect burnout but I'm not sure how to approach the conversation without sounding accusatory. How should I handle this?"*

AI suggests empathetic approaches.

Level up:

"Draft an opening line for that conversation that's supportive, not confrontational."

"What questions should I ask to understand the root cause?"

"If they admit they're overwhelmed, what solutions can I offer?"

"Role-play with me. You be the employee. I'll practice the conversation. After I respond, tell me what I could improve."

What you're learning: Emotional intelligence, communication strategies, leadership skills.

The pilot move: Practice the conversation with AI, but remember real humans are unpredictable. Adapt in the moment based on what you observe.

** ** **

The Art of the Follow-Up Question

This is what separates pilots from passengers.

Passengers accept AI's first answer.
Pilots dig deeper.

Here are the follow-up questions that unlock deeper learning:

When AI gives you a list:
→ *"Expand on #3. Why is that particularly important?"*

When AI gives you a strategy:
→ *"What would cause this strategy to fail?"*

When AI explains a concept:
→ *"Explain it again, but for someone with zero background knowledge."*
→ *"Now explain it using an analogy."*

When AI gives you advice:
→ *"What would the opposite advice be? When would that be better?"*

When you're skeptical:
→ *"Are you sure about this? What evidence supports it?"*
→ *"What am I missing that would change this conclusion?"*

When you want to learn:
→ *"Teach me the underlying principle so I can apply this in other situations."*
The pattern: Every answer should spark a new question.

If you're not asking follow-ups, you're not learning you're just consuming.

The Daily Practice: Build Your AI Fluency

You can't become fluent in a language by using it once a week. Same with AI.

Here's a 30-day challenge to build genuine competency:

Week 1: Exploration

- **Day 1-2:** Use AI for small tasks (emails, summaries, brainstorming)
- **Day 3-4:** Experiment with different prompting styles see what changes the output
- **Day 5-7:** Pick one area of your job and use AI daily for it

Week 2: Iteration

- **Day 8-10:** Never accept AI's first response. Always refine at least twice
- **Day 11-13:** Use AI to learn something new outside your expertise (a topic, a skill)
- **Day 14:** Reflect on what prompts worked best and why

Week 3: Integration

- **Day 15-17:** Build a workflow where AI handles one repetitive task automatically
- **Day 18-20:** Use AI to improve a core skill (writing, presenting, analyzing)

- **Day 21:** Compare your work with and without AI what's different?

Week 4: Mastery

- **Day 22-24:** Teach someone else how to use AI effectively
- **Day 25-27:** Use AI to tackle your most complex work problem
- **Day 28-29:** Challenge yourself to use AI in an unusual way (creative experimentation)
- **Day 30:** Audit your progress what changed in how you work?

By day 30, you'll know more about practical AI use than 95% of the workforce.

** ** **

The Red Flags: When You're Using AI Wrong

Watch for these warning signs:

You can't explain AI's output in your own words
→ You're copying, not learning

You feel anxious when AI isn't available
→ You've become dependent
You never disagree with AI's suggestions
→ You're not thinking critically

Your work all sounds the same (and generic)

→ AI is replacing your voice, not enhancing it

You stop fact-checking
→ You're trusting blindly
You skip the "why" and jump straight to the "what"
→ You're prioritizing speed over understanding

If you catch yourself doing any of these, pause. Reset. Remember: AI is a tool for amplification, not replacement.

** ** **

The Green Flags: When You're Using AI Right

Celebrate these signs of healthy AI use:

You catch AI's errors before they cause problems
→ Your judgment is sharp

Your outputs have your unique voice and perspective
→ AI enhances, but you lead

You can do the work without AI just slower
→ AI speeds you up, doesn't prop you up

You're learning new skills faster than before
→ AI is a tutor, not a crutch

You ask better questions than you did a month ago
→ You're improving, not stagnating

You use AI to explore ideas you wouldn't have considered
→ AI expands your thinking

When you're hitting these green flags, you're in the sweet spot. Keep going.

** ** **

The Ultimate Skill: Learning How to Learn

Here's the meta-lesson of this chapter:

The most valuable skill in the AI era isn't knowing how to use a specific tool. It's knowing how to learn anything, rapidly, using AI as your tutor.

Because the tools will change. ChatGPT today, something else tomorrow.

But if you master the learning loop if you know how to ask questions, iterate, challenge outputs, synthesize knowledge, and apply it you'll adapt to whatever comes next.

You're not learning AI. You're learning how to learn with AI.

That's the skill that never goes obsolete.

The Mindset Shift

Stop thinking: *"What can AI do for me?"*

Start thinking: *"What can I learn by working with AI?"*

Stop thinking: *"AI will save me time."*
Start thinking: *"AI will help me get better."*

Stop thinking: *"I need to understand how AI works."*

Start thinking: *"I need to understand how to think with AI."*

That shift from tool to partner, from shortcut to teacher is everything.

CHAPTER 5 EXERCISE:
YOUR FIRST LEARNING PROJECT

This week, pick ONE skill you want to improve something related to your work that you've been meaning to get better at.

It could be:

- Giving presentations
- Writing persuasively
- Analyzing data
- Managing conflict
- Designing visuals
- Understanding finance
- Negotiating deals

Day 1: Ask AI to create a learning plan. *"I want to get better at [skill]. I have 30 minutes a day. Create a 2-week learning plan with daily exercises."*
Day 2-13: Follow the plan. Use AI as your tutor. Ask questions. Practice. Get feedback from AI.

Day 14: Assess your progress. What improved? Where did AI help most? Where did you still need human guidance?

Bonus: At the end, teach someone else what you learned. If you can teach it, you truly learned it.

Next Chapter Preview:
Chapter 6 – AI in the Workplace: Real Stories of People Who Adapted (And Thrived)

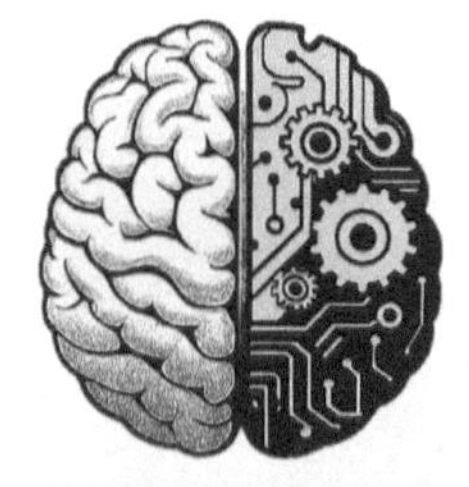

Chapter 6

AI in the Workplace

Rachel was drowning.

As a solo immigration lawyer running her own practice, she was working 70-hour weeks and still falling behind. Client consultations, legal research, document preparation, court filings, emails, phone calls everything bottlenecked at her.

She'd built a good reputation. Referrals were steady. But she couldn't scale. She couldn't hire an associate margins were too thin. She couldn't raise prices her clients were already stretched.

She was trapped between success and burnout.

Then, in January 2024, a colleague mentioned ChatGPT. Rachel was skeptical. *"AI can't practice law,"* she thought. And she was right.

But AI could do almost everything around practicing law.

Within six months, Rachel had transformed her practice. She wasn't working less she was working on completely different things. And her revenue had increased 40% while her stress had plummeted.

This is her story. And the stories of five other professionals who saw AI not as a threat, but as the leverage they'd been waiting for.

Story 1: The Solo Lawyer Who Got Her Life Back

Rachel Martinez, Immigration Attorney | Austin, Texas

The Before

Rachel's typical day started at 6 AM and ended at 8 PM. Her inbox had 200+ unread messages. Client intake forms sat in her queue for days. She spent hours drafting petitions that followed nearly identical templates but required manual customization for each case.

"I became a lawyer to help people," she told me. *"But I was spending 80% of my time on paperwork and 20% actually counseling clients. It was backwards."*

The Shift

Rachel started small. She used ChatGPT to draft client response emails not the legal advice itself, but the explanatory language around it.

Before AI:
Writing an email explaining visa timelines: 20 minutes

With AI:

Prompt: *"Draft a compassionate email explaining to a client that their H-1B visa process will take 6-8 months. Address common concerns about job security and family planning. Professional but warm tone."*
Edit AI's draft to add case-specific details: 5 minutes

Time saved per email: 15 minutes
Emails per day: 10-15
Time saved daily: 2.5 hours

Then she got bolder.

She created a system where AI drafted initial versions of common legal documents:

- Visa petition letters
- Responses to RFEs (Request for Evidence)
- Client intake summaries
- Case status updates

Her rule: AI drafts, she reviews and personalizes.

"I never send AI-generated content without thorough review," she emphasizes. *"But starting from an 80% draft instead of a blank page changed everything."*

The Results (6 Months Later)

- **Client capacity increased from 30 to 45 active cases**
- **Response time dropped from 48 hours to 4 hours**
- **Revenue up 40% (more clients, same overhead)**
- **Working hours down from 70 to 50 per week**
- **Client satisfaction scores improved (faster responses, more personal attention during consultations)**

What She Learned

"The first month, I was terrified of making mistakes. I over-edited everything AI produced. But I realized I was catching errors because I was reviewing carefully something I sometimes rushed through when I wrote everything myself.

AI didn't make me lazy. It made me more thorough because I had the time and energy to be thorough."

Rachel's Advice

"Use AI for repetitive work, not novel legal reasoning. Draft the hundredth visa letter with AI. But when you're arguing a unique legal point or counseling a client through a difficult decision? That's all you. The goal isn't to work less it's to spend your time on the work that actually requires your expertise."

Story 2: The Teacher Who Became a Curriculum Designer

Marcus Webb, 7th Grade Science Teacher | Portland, Oregon

The Before

Marcus loved teaching. He hated the administrative burden.

Lesson planning. Creating differentiated materials for students at different reading levels. Parent emails. Grading assignments. Designing quizzes. Writing progress reports.

"By the time I finished preparing for class, I was too exhausted to be present during class," he said.

The Shift

Marcus started using AI as a curriculum assistant.

Example: Photosynthesis Lesson

Old process:

- Research engaging examples: 45 minutes
- Create lesson outline: 30 minutes
- Design three versions (advanced, standard, remedial): 90 minutes

- Create visual aids: 60 minutes
- Write quiz questions: 30 minutes
- **Total: 4 hours**

New process:

- **Prompt AI:** *"Create a 50-minute lesson plan on photosynthesis for 7th graders. Include: a compelling hook using real-world examples, a clear explanation using analogies, three different versions (advanced, on-level, and struggling readers), five quiz questions at varying difficulty, and a hands-on activity. Address the common misconception that plants only photosynthesize during the day."*
- Review output, customize for his specific students: 45 minutes
- **Total: 45 minutes**

Time saved: 3+ hours per lesson

But Marcus didn't just save time. He got better.

"AI exposed me to teaching strategies I hadn't considered. It suggested analogies I wouldn't have thought of. It reminded me of misconceptions I'd forgotten to address. I was learning pedagogy while I worked."

The Results (One School Year)

- **Lesson quality improved** (peer reviews, student feedback)
- **Saved 10-12 hours per week** on planning and administrative work
- **Used extra time for:** one-on-one student tutoring, professional development, developing a new elective course
- **Student test scores:** Up 12% (correlation, not causation but worth noting)
- **Teacher burnout assessment:** Dropped from "high risk" to "moderate"

The Unexpected Win

"I started sharing my AI-generated lesson plans with other teachers. I created a template system. Now five teachers in my department use the same approach. We're collaborating more, customizing less from scratch. It raised the floor for all of us."

Marcus's Advice

"Don't use AI to do less teaching. Use it to do more teaching and less paperwork. The algorithm can generate a worksheet. Only you can see when a student's eyes light up with understanding and know exactly how to build on that moment. Automate the prep so you can be fully present for the magic."

Story 3: The Entrepreneur Who Launched Faster

Kira Patel, Founder of GreenThread Apparel | Chicago, Illinois

The Before

Kira had a vision: sustainable activewear made from recycled materials, targeted at environmentally conscious millennials.

She had fashion design experience. She had supplier connections. She had savings to invest.

What she didn't have: marketing expertise, business planning knowledge, or time to get an MBA.

She was stuck in analysis paralysis. *"I spent six months researching how to launch. I kept thinking I needed to learn more before I could start."*

The Shift

Her friend, a startup founder, gave her blunt advice: *"Stop researching. Start building. Use AI to fill your knowledge gaps."*

Kira created an AI advisory board.

AI as Marketing Strategist: *"I'm launching a sustainable activewear brand. Target demographic: environmentally conscious women aged 25-40. Product differentiation: recycled materials, carbon-neutral shipping. Budget: $15,000 for first six months. Create a customer acquisition strategy with specific channels, budget allocation, and success metrics."*

AI as Financial Analyst: *"Build a financial model for my first year. Assumptions: $120 retail price per item, $45 COGS, 5% conversion rate on website traffic, $25 customer acquisition cost. Show me break-even analysis and cash flow projections."*

AI as Brand Strategist: *"Generate 20 brand name ideas that convey: sustainability, movement, freshness, modern femininity. Avoid clichés like 'eco' or 'green."*

She didn't blindly follow AI's advice. She researched. She validated. She consulted real humans other founders, a part-time marketing consultant, her accountant.

But AI compressed her learning curve from months to weeks.

The Results (First Year)

- **Launched in 3 months** instead of projected 9-12 months
- **Revenue: $180,000** in first year (profitable month 8)
- **Customer acquisition cost:** 15% below industry average (AI's strategy worked)

- **Time saved on business planning, market research, content creation:** Estimated 400+ hours

The Mistake She Made (And Fixed)

"Month three, I got lazy. I let AI write all my Instagram captions. My engagement tanked. People could tell it wasn't authentic.

I learned: AI can draft, but your voice has to shine through. Now I use AI for first drafts and outlines, but I rewrite everything in my own voice. Engagement recovered within two weeks."

Kira's Advice

"As a founder, you're wearing 10 hats. You can't be an expert in everything. AI lets you be competent in everything while you focus on being excellent at your core strength. I'm a designer, not a marketer. AI gave me a marketing IQ boost without getting an MBA. But I still hired real consultants for critical decisions. Use AI to learn fast, but validate with humans who've done it before.

Story 4: The Sales Rep Who Became a Top Performer

David Chen, Enterprise SaaS Sales | San Francisco, California

The Before

David was a mid-tier sales rep at a B2B software company. Good, not great. He hit quota most quarters but rarely exceeded it.

His weakness: personalization at scale.

Top performers sent highly customized outreach to prospects researching their company, referencing recent news, tailoring the pitch. It worked, but it was time-intensive.

David's approach: semi-generic templates with minor customization. Faster, but lower response rates.

"I knew personalization mattered, but I had 100+ prospects in my pipeline. I couldn't spend an hour researching each one."

The Shift

David built an AI-powered research and outreach system.

Step 1: Research

- Input: Prospect's company name and LinkedIn profile
- AI prompt: *"Research [Company Name]. Summarize: recent news, growth challenges in their industry, tech stack (if public), potential pain points our product solves. Keep it under 200 words."*
- Time: 2 minutes (vs. 20 minutes manual research)

Step 2: Personalized Outreach

- AI prompt: *"Draft a cold email to [Name], [Title] at [Company]. Our product helps companies like theirs [specific benefit]. Reference [recent company news from research]. Tone: conversational, helpful (not salesy), under 100 words, clear call to action: 15-minute intro call."*
- David edits for voice and accuracy: 3 minutes
- Time: 5 minutes total (vs. 15 minutes per email)

Step 3: Follow-Up Sequence

- AI generates 4-email sequence with different angles
- David selects the best two, refines them
- Time: 10 minutes (vs. 40 minutes)

The Results (6 Months)

- **Response rate:** Increased from 8% to 18%
- **Meetings booked:** Up 120%
- **Deals closed:** Increased from 12 to 22 per quarter

- **Exceeded quota:** 5 of 6 quarters
- **Promotion:** Named Senior Account Executive
- **Income:** Up 35% (base salary + commission)

The Pushback He Faced

"My manager accused me of using AI to 'cheat.' I had to show him my process. I wasn't automating relationship-building I was automating research. The actual conversations, the discovery calls, the negotiations? All me. I just showed up to those conversations better prepared and with more prospects than before.
Once he understood that, he had me train the whole team."

David's Advice

"In sales, relationships are everything. AI can't build relationships only you can. But AI can help you show up to every interaction with better research, better talking points, and better follow-through. I went from 'spray and pray' to 'strategic and personalized' without hiring a research assistant. The prospects feel it. They respond better because I'm not wasting their time with generic pitches."

Story 5: The Designer Who Doubled Her Output

Alicia Rodriguez, Freelance Graphic Designer | Austin, Texas

The Before

Alicia was talented but overwhelmed. She had more client requests than she could handle, but she couldn't raise rates she was already at market rate for freelancers in her area.
Her bottleneck: the early conceptual phase.

"Clients would say, 'We want a logo that feels modern but warm.' I'd spend hours sketching concepts, many of which went nowhere. By the time I found the right direction, I'd burned 10-15 hours."

The Shift

Alicia started using AI (Midjourney, ChatGPT, and Adobe Firefly) for concept exploration.

New Process:

Phase 1: Concept Generation (with ChatGPT)

- Client brief: *"Modern but warm logo for a family-owned coffee roaster"*

- Prompt: *"Generate 15 logo concept directions for a family-owned coffee roaster. The brand values are: warmth, tradition, quality, community. Mix literal and abstract concepts."*
- Output: 15 written concepts
- Time: 5 minutes

Phase 2: Visual Exploration (with Midjourney)

- Select 5 strongest written concepts
- Generate visual variations for each
- Present to client as mood board
- Time: 30 minutes

Phase 3: Refinement (Human Designer Work)

- Client selects direction
- Alicia sketches, refines, perfects in Illustrator
- This is where her expertise and taste shine
- Time: 8-10 hours

Old process: 18-20 hours total
New process: 10-12 hours total
Time saved: 40-50%

The Results (One Year)

- **Client capacity:** Increased from 8 to 14 per month
- **Revenue:** Up 60% (more clients, same rates)
- **Client satisfaction:** Improved (more concepts to choose from, faster turnaround)
- **Creative quality:** Better (more time for refinement, less time staring at blank canvas)

The Ethical Dilemma She Faced

"I felt guilty at first. Was I 'cheating'? Was AI doing the creative work?

Then I realized: AI generates ideas. I make them beautiful. The concepts AI produces are generic until I apply my taste, my typography skills, my understanding of the client's brand.

I'm not a worse designer for using AI. I'm a more efficient designer. And my clients get better results because I'm spending my energy on the craft, not the brainstorming slog."

Alicia's Advice

"AI is a brainstorming partner, not a replacement for your creative eye. Use it to get past the blank page. Use it to explore directions you wouldn't have considered. But the final 20% the refinement, the taste, the 'this feels right' that's all you. Clients hire you for your judgment, not for idea generation. AI makes you faster. Your taste makes you valuable."

Story 6: The Manager Who Built a Better Team

Terrance Johnson, Operations Manager | Seattle, Washington

The Before

Terrance managed a team of 15 customer support specialists at a mid-sized SaaS company. Turnover was high. Morale was low. Onboarding new hires took 6-8 weeks before they were productive.

"I was firefighting constantly. I didn't have time to mentor. I didn't have time to build systems. I was just reacting."

The Shift

Terrance used AI to systematize knowledge and reduce repetitive management tasks.

Initiative #1: AI-Powered Onboarding

- Created a ChatGPT-based internal knowledge base
- New hires could ask: *"How do I handle a billing dispute?"* or *"What's our policy on refunds after 30 days?"*
- AI provided answers based on company documentation
- Time to productivity: Dropped from 6-8 weeks to 3-4 weeks

Initiative 2: Performance Coaching

- Used AI to analyze support ticket data and identify coaching opportunities
- Prompt: *"Analyze this team member's last 50 tickets. Identify patterns: response time, resolution rate, customer satisfaction scores. Suggest specific coaching points."*
- Terrance reviewed AI's analysis, added context, delivered personalized feedback
- Coaching quality improved (data-driven, specific)

Initiative 3: Meeting Preparation

- Before 1-on-1s, used AI to prepare discussion points
- Prompt: *"I'm meeting with [team member]. Recent performance metrics: [data]. Known challenges: [context]. Suggest three discussion topics that balance support and accountability."*
- Meetings became more productive, less improvisational

The Results (One Year)

- **Turnover decreased from 35% to 18%**
- **Employee satisfaction scores: Up 28%**
- **New hire productivity timeline:** Cut in half
- **Terrance's time spent on repetitive questions:** Down 60%
- **Time reinvested in:** Strategic planning, team development, process improvement
- **Promotion:** Named Director of Customer Experience

What Surprised Him

"I thought AI would make management more robotic. The opposite happened. By automating the routine stuff, I had more time for genuine human connection. I could actually listen in 1-on-1s instead of mentally running through my task list. I became a better manager because I used AI, not despite it."

Terrance's Advice

"Management is about people, not processes. But processes eat up the time you need for people. Use AI to handle the processes documentation, data analysis, scheduling, routine communication so you can spend your energy on what matters: coaching, mentoring, building trust, solving complex human problems. The best use of AI in management isn't replacing human judgment. It's freeing you up to exercise more of it."

** ** **

The Common Threads

Six people. Six industries. Six different challenges.

But notice the patterns:

1. They didn't use AI to do less work. They used it to do different work.

Rachel didn't reduce her caseload she increased it and spent more time on complex legal reasoning.

Marcus didn't teach fewer classes he spent more time with struggling students.

Kira didn't avoid learning business she learned faster.

2. They stayed in control.

None of them blindly trusted AI. They reviewed. They edited. They validated. They added judgment.

AI was the co-pilot. They were always the pilot.

3. They experimented without fear.

They didn't wait for the perfect use case. They tried things. They failed. They adjusted.

David's first AI-written emails bombed. He learned why and got better.

4. They protected their core value.

Rachel: Legal judgment
Marcus: Teaching presence
Kira: Design vision
David: Relationship-building
Alicia: Creative taste
Terrance: Leadership and empathy

They used AI to handle everything around their core value so they could double down on what made them irreplaceable.

5. They became advocates.

Once they saw results, they didn't hoard the knowledge. They taught others.
Marcus trained his department. David trained his sales team. Terrance built systems for his whole team.

Because people who thrive with AI aren't threatened by others using it. They know the real differentiator is how you use it, not whether you use it.

** ** **

What These Stories Mean for You

You don't need to be in tech. You don't need to be young. You don't need to be *"naturally good with technology."*

You just need to be willing to experiment.

Every person in this chapter started as a skeptic or a beginner. They didn't have special skills. They had curiosity and a problem they wanted to solve.

That's the profile of an AI success story: someone with a problem and the willingness to try something new.

That can be you.

CHAPTER 6 EXERCISE: FIND YOUR RACHEL/MARCUS/KIRA MOMENT

This week, identify your biggest time-drain at work.

Step 1: Track your time for three days. What task do you keep doing that feels repetitive and draining?

Step 2: Ask yourself: "Could AI do 70-80% of this?"

Step 3: Experiment. Try using AI to handle that task for one week.

Step 4: Measure the results. Time saved? Quality maintained? What did you learn?

Step 5: Refine your approach. What worked? What didn't? How can you improve the process?

Step 6: Teach someone else what you learned.

Your transformation doesn't have to be dramatic. It starts with one task, one experiment, one small win Then you build from there.

Next Chapter Preview:
Chapter 7 – Lifelong Learning in the AI Era: How to Stay Ahead When Everything Keeps Changing

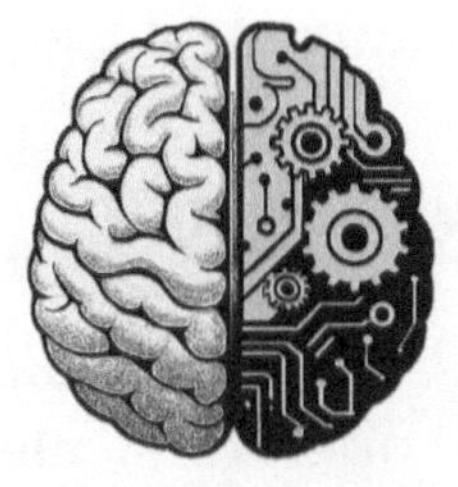

Chapter 7

Lifelong Learning in the AI Era

In 1930, the economist John Maynard Keynes made a bold prediction: by 2030, technological progress would be so advanced that people would only need to work 15 hours per week.

He was right about the technology. We have machines that can do in seconds what took humans days.

He was wrong about the work.

We didn't work less. We worked *differently*. The jobs of 1930 switchboard operators, elevator attendants, typists disappeared. New jobs emerged: software developers, digital marketers, data scientists, UX designers.

The pattern holds: **technology doesn't reduce the need for human work. It changes what that work looks like.**

But here's what Keynes couldn't have predicted: **the pace of that change would keep accelerating.**

In 1930, you could learn a skill and use it for 40 years. By 1980, maybe 20 years. By 2000, maybe 10 years.

Today? Some skills become outdated in 2-3 years.

The half-life of skills is shrinking. And it's not slowing down.

The New Career Reality

Let me paint you two futures.

Future A: The Static Professional

Jamie graduated in 2015 with a marketing degree. She learned SEO, Facebook ads, content marketing. She got good at those things. Really good.

By 2025, her skills are still valuable but less so. The algorithms changed. The platforms evolved. New channels emerged (TikTok, AI-generated content, voice search). Her expertise is stuck in 2015.

She's not incompetent. She's just *outdated*. Younger professionals who learned the new tools are outperforming her. Employers hesitate to hire her they see someone who stopped learning.

She feels the gap widening but doesn't know how to close it. She's busy working. She doesn't have time to learn new things. The cycle perpetuates.

By 2030, she's struggling to find work that pays what she's used to.

Future B: The Adaptive Professional

Jordan graduated the same year, same degree. But Jordan treats every year like freshman year.

She dedicates 5 hours per week to learning. She experiments with new platforms before they're mainstream. When AI tools emerge, she's an early adopter. When algorithms change, she studies why.

She's not smarter than Jamie. She's just committed to *continuous learning* as a core part of her identity.

By 2025, she's a sought-after expert. Not because she knows everything, but because she's proven she can *learn anything*. Employers see someone who stays ahead of change.

By 2030, she's leading teams, speaking at conferences, consulting. Her career trajectory isn't linear it's exponential.

> ## LEADER PERSPECTIVE
> *"We will all operate at a little bit higher of a level of abstraction. We will all have access to a lot more capability. We'll still make decisions. They may trend more towards curation over time, but we'll make decisions about what should happen in the world."*
> **Sam Altman, OpenAI CEO**

This describes the shift happening right now. Your value is moving from *how fast you can complete tasks to how well you can evaluate options and make choices*. From execution to judgment. From processing to curating.

The difference between Jamie and Jordan isn't talent. It's mindset.

Jamie sees learning as something you do before your career.

Jordan sees learning as something you do during your career.

In the AI era, Jordan's mindset isn't optional. It's survival.

** ** **

The Half-Life Problem

In nuclear physics, half-life is the time it takes for a substance to lose half its radioactivity.

In the workplace, **skill half-life** is the time it takes for your knowledge to become half as valuable.

And it's plummeting.

A 2018 study by IBM found that the half-life of technical skills has dropped from 10-15 years in the 1980s to **2.5 years** today.

Think about that.

Half of what you know about your job will be obsolete or significantly less valuable in 30 months.

This isn't just true for tech workers. It's true for everyone.

- Teachers: Pedagogy evolves. EdTech tools change. Student learning styles shift.

- **Healthcare workers:** New treatments emerge. Protocols update. Medical knowledge doubles every 73 days.
- **Marketers:** Platforms rise and fall. Consumer behavior shifts. Attribution models change.
- **Lawyers:** Regulations update. Case law evolves. Legal tech advances.

The question isn't whether your skills will become outdated. **It's whether you'll update them faster than they decay.**

** ** **

The Adaptability Advantage

Here's the good news: **adaptability is a skill you can build.**

It's not a personality trait you're born with. It's a muscle you develop through practice.

And in the AI era, it's the meta-skill that makes every other skill more durable.

Think of it this way:

- **Old model:** Learn a skill → Use it for decades → Retire
- **New model:** Learn how to learn → Apply to Skill A → When Skill A becomes obsolete, rapidly learn Skill B → Repeat

The most valuable professionals aren't the ones who know the most. They're the ones who learn the fastest.

** ** **

The Three Layers of Learning

Not all learning is created equal. There are three levels, and most people get stuck at Level 1.

Level 1: Content Learning

This is learning *facts and procedures.*

- *"How do I use Excel's VLOOKUP function?"*
- *"What are the Facebook ad specs?"*
- *"How do I file this legal form?"*

Value: High in the short term. This is what gets immediate work done.

Problem: Highly perishable. When the tool changes, this knowledge becomes useless.

Most professional development stops here. You learn the tool. You use the tool. The tool changes. You're behind.

Level 2: Principle Learning

This is learning why things work.

- *"Why does this marketing message resonate with this audience?"*
- *"Why does this teaching method work better for visual learners?"*
- *"Why does this financial model assume these growth rates?"*

Value: Medium-to-long term. Principles outlast specific tools.

Advantage: When tools change, you can apply the same principles to new tools.

Example: A marketer who understands persuasion psychology can adapt when platforms change. The psychology doesn't change just the medium.

Level 3: Learning How to Learn

This is **meta-learning** learning about the learning process itself.

- *"How do I identify the core concepts in a new domain?"*
- *"What's my most effective learning style?"*
- *"How do I validate whether I've truly learned something?"*
- *"How do I learn complex skills quickly?"*

Value: Infinite. This is the skill that never becomes obsolete.

Advantage: You can enter any new domain and get competent quickly.

This is the layer most professionals ignore. And it's the layer that separates those who thrive from those who survive.

** ** **

The Continuous Learning System

So how do you actually do this? How do you stay ahead when everything keeps changing?

Here's a practical system used by the most adaptable professionals:

Component 1: The Curiosity Budget

Most people allocate time for work, but not for *learning*.

Adaptive professionals flip this.

The Rule: Dedicate 5-10% of your work week to learning that has no immediate application.

- 40-hour week = 2-4 hours of learning time
- Not training for your current job. Learning adjacent skills, emerging trends, or completely unrelated domains.

Why this works:

Cross-domain knowledge creates competitive advantage. The designer who studies psychology. The engineer who learns sales. The teacher who understands data analysis.

Practical application:

- **1 hour:** Read articles, watch tutorials, explore new tools
- **1 hour:** Take an online course or watch expert talks
1 hour: Experiment hands-on with something new
1 hour: Reflect and document what you learned

The ROI: In 1 year, you'll have 100-200 hours of learning. That's roughly 2-3 college courses worth of knowledge. Compounded over 10 years? You'll have expertise in 5-6 new domains.

Component 2: The Learning Sprint

When a new skill becomes critical, don't dabble. Sprint.

The Method: Dedicate 30 days to intensive learning in one specific area.

Week 1: Foundations

- Consume beginner content (courses, books, videos)
- Build a basic mental model of the domain
- Identify the core concepts

Week 2: Application

- Practice daily
- Use AI as a tutor (ask questions, get feedback)
- Build something small using the skill

Week 3: Feedback

- Get expert review (hire a coach, join a community, post your work)
- Identify gapsFocus practice on weak areas

Week 4: Teaching

- Write a blog post explaining what you learned
- Teach a colleague
- Create a resource for others

Why teaching matters: You don't truly understand something until you can explain it simply. Teaching forces clarity.

Real example:

Sarah, a project manager, needed to learn basic data analysis. She dedicated 30 days:

- Week 1: Took a free SQL course on Khan Academy
- Week 2: Analyzed her team's project data using SQL
- Week 3: Had a data analyst friend review her queries and suggest improvements
- Week 4: Taught her team how to pull their own reports

After 30 days, she wasn't a data scientist. But she was competent capable of having informed conversations and doing basic analysis. That competence opened doors.

Component 3: The Signal Detection System

You can't learn everything. You need to prioritize *what* to learn.

The skill: Learn to distinguish signal (valuable emerging trends) from noise (fleeting hype).

As Jeff Bezos recently observed about the current AI boom: *"Every experiment gets funded. Every company gets funded. The good ideas and the bad ideas. And investors have a hard time in the middle of this excitement distinguishing between the good ideas and the bad ideas."*

This same challenge applies to you. Not every AI tool deserves your time. Not every trend deserves your attention. You need a filter.

How to detect signals:

Ask these questions:

- **Is this solving a real problem that's getting worse?**
  (Yes = signal. No = maybe noise.)
- **Are serious people investing in this?**
  (If major companies, investors, or respected experts are doubling down, pay attention.)
- **Is adoption accelerating?**
  (Check Google Trends, job postings, course enrollments. Exponential growth = signal.)
- **Will this still matter in 3 years?**
  (If unclear, it's probably noise.)

Example in action:

2021: NFTs exploded. Hype everywhere.

Signal or noise?

- Problem solved? Vague. Mostly speculation.
- Serious investment? Some, but mostly retail investors.
- Adoption accelerating? Temporarily, then crashed.
- Still matter in 3 years? Unclear.

Verdict: Noise for most professionals. Watch, but don't dedicate serious learning time.

2022: AI (ChatGPT) exploded.

Signal or noise?

- Problem solved? Yes. Real productivity gains across industries.
- Serious investment? Massive. Microsoft, Google, every major tech company.
- Adoption accelerating? Yes. Exponential user growth.
- Still matter in 3 years? Almost certainly.

Verdict: Strong signal. Prioritize learning.

The goal: Spend your learning time on signals, ignore the noise.

Component 4: The Deliberate Practice Loop

Learning isn't just consuming information. It's *doing + feedback + refinement.*

The Loop:

1. **Attempt the skill** (even if you're bad at it)
2. **Get feedback** (from AI, mentors, peers, or data)
3. **Identify specific weaknesses**
4. **Practice those weaknesses deliberately**
5. **Repeat**

Example: Learning to write better marketing copy

- **Attempt:** Write a product landing page
- **Feedback:** Ask ChatGPT: "Critique this landing page. What's weak? What's confusing? What's missing?"
- **Identify:** Headline is vague, CTA is buried, no social proof
- **Practice:** Rewrite headline 10 different ways. Study high-converting landing pages.
- **Repeat:** Rewrite the page. Get feedback again.

The key difference:

- **Passive learning:** Read about copywriting
- **Deliberate practice:** Write, get critiqued, rewrite, repeat

Deliberate practice is 10x more effective. And with AI, you have instant feedback on demand.

Component 5: The Knowledge Capture System

You'll forget 90% of what you learn unless you document it.

The solution: Build a personal knowledge management system.

Options:
- **Notion** (flexible, visual)
- **Obsidian** (networked note-taking)
- **Evernote** (simple, searchable)
- **Google Docs** (free, collaborative)

What to capture:

- Key insights from articles, courses, conversations
- Lessons from mistakes
- Frameworks and mental models
- Resources you want to revisit

The method:

After learning something valuable, write:

1. **What did I learn?** (in your own words)
2. **Why does it matter?**
3. **How will I apply it?**

Why this works: Writing forces synthesis. Reviewing old notes reveals patterns. Your knowledge base becomes searchable.

Pro tip: Review your notes monthly. Update them. Delete outdated ideas. This keeps your knowledge current.

** ** **

The Mindset Shifts That Matter

Systems are helpful. But mindset is fundamental.

Here are the mental shifts that separate continuous learners from everyone else:

Shift 1: From *"I Don't Know"* to *"I Don't Know Yet"*

Fixed mindset: *"I'm not good with technology."*
Growth mindset: *"I'm not good with technology yet, but I can learn."*

That one word yet changes everything. It reframes inability as temporary, not permanent.

Shift 2: From Expertise to Curiosity

Old identity: *"I'm an expert in X."*
New identity: *"I'm someone who learns rapidly."*

When your identity is tied to specific expertise, you resist change. When it's tied to learning, you welcome it.

Shift 3: From Perfectionism to Iteration

Perfectionist: *"I need to fully understand this before I try it."*

Iterative learner: *"I'll learn by doing. I'll make mistakes. I'll improve."*

Perfectionism paralyzes. Iteration accelerates.

The 80/20 rule: Get 80% competent quickly, then refine over time. Don't wait for 100% before you start.

Shift 4: From Scarcity to Abundance

Scarcity mindset: *"If others learn this skill, I'll have more competition."*

Abundance mindset: *"If others learn this skill, I'll have better collaborators."*
Adaptive people share knowledge freely. They know the real differentiator isn't *what* you know it's how fast you learn next.

Shift 5: From Comfort to Challenge

Comfort-seeking: *"I'll stick with what I know."*

Challenge-seeking: *"I'll deliberately put myself in situations where I feel incompetent."*

Growth happens at the edge of your comfort zone. Seek discomfort. It's where learning lives.

** ** **

The Career Insurance Policy

Here's a reframe that makes continuous learning easier:

Don't think of learning as optional professional development.

Think of it as career insurance.

You pay for car insurance hoping you'll never need it. You pay for health insurance as a safety net.

Learning is the same it's insurance against obsolescence.

Every hour you spend learning is an investment in your future employability, adaptability, and peace of mind.

And unlike other insurance, this one pays dividends even if you never face a crisis. You get smarter, more capable, more confident.

The cost: 5-10% of your time.

The return: Career resilience for decades.

That's a bargain.

** ** **

The Compounding Effect

Here's the math that makes continuous learning irresistible:

If you improve 1% per week through deliberate learning, you're **67% better after one year.**

If you improve 1% per week for 5 years, you're 1,200% better than when you started.

This is compound interest for your brain.

Most people don't see it because the daily improvement is invisible. But over years? The gap between continuous learners and static professionals becomes a chasm.

How to Future-Proof Your Career

Here's your practical action plan:

This Month:

- **Audit your skills.** What's becoming outdated? What's emerging?
- **Set a curiosity budget.** Block 2-4 hours per week for learning.
- **Pick one signal to chase.** What's the most important emerging skill in your field?
- **Start a knowledge capture system.** Choose a tool. Start documenting.

This Quarter:

- **Complete a learning sprint.** 30 days, one focused skill.
- **Get feedback.** Find someone better than you. Ask for critique.
- **Teach something.** Write a post, mentor a colleague, explain what you learned.

This Year:

- **Repeat.** Four learning sprints = four new competencies per year.
- **Review and refine.** What worked? What didn't? Improve your process.
- **Build a reputation as a learner.** Share insights, help others, become known for growth.

In 5 years, you'll be a different professional. Not because you worked harder. Because you learned smarter.

** ** **

The Ultimate Question

At the end of your career 20, 30, 40 years from now what will you wish you'd learned?

You won't regret the things you tried and failed at. You'll regret the things you were too scared or too comfortable to try.

The AI era rewards the courageous learner. The one who says, *"I don't know this yet, but I'll figure it out."*

That person doesn't fear change. They architect it.

Be that person.

CHAPTER 7 EXERCISE:
BUILD YOUR LEARNING SYSTEM

This week, create your continuous learning infrastructure:

Day 1: Audit

- List 10 skills you use regularly at work
- Rate each: Stable (won't change much) or Decaying (will be outdated soon)
- Identify the top 3 skills you need to upgrade or acquire

Day 2: Budget

- Block 2 hours on your calendar for learning, every week, for the next 3 months
- Treat it like a meeting with your future self non-negotiable

Day 3: Capture

- Choose a knowledge management tool (Notion, Obsidian, Google Docs)
- Create your first note: "What I want to learn this year"

Day 4: Sprint Plan

- Pick ONE skill from your audit
- Plan a 30-day learning sprint: what will you learn each week?

Day 5: Signal Detection

- Subscribe to 2-3 sources that cover emerging trends in your industry
- Set up Google Alerts for key topics

Day 6: First Practice

- Spend 30 minutes practicing your chosen skill
- Document what you learned and what you struggled with

Day 7: Reflect

- Review the week. What worked? What felt hard?
- Adjust your plan for next week.

By the end of the week, you'll have a functioning learning system. By the end of the month, you'll have a new skill. By the end of the year, you'll have transformed your career.

Next Chapter Preview:
Chapter 8 – A Balanced Future: Leading AI, Not Following It

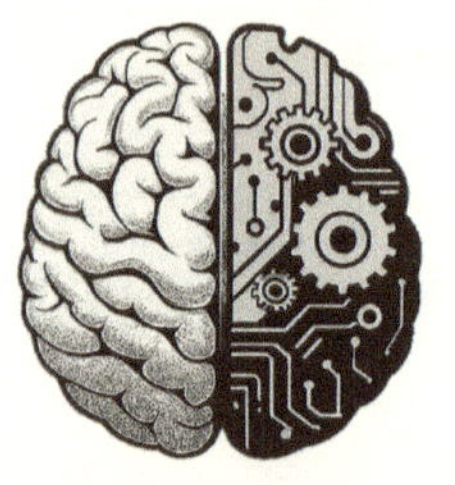

Chapter 8

A Balanced Future

In 1997, IBM's Deep Blue defeated world chess champion Garry Kasparov.

The headlines screamed: *"Man vs. Machine: The End of Human Chess Supremacy."*

Kasparov was devastated. But a year later, he had a radical idea.

What if humans and computers played together?

He organized the first *"freestyle chess"* tournament teams could be human-only, AI-only, or human-AI hybrids. The format was simple: anything goes. Use any tools, any strategy, any combination.

Who won?

Not the grandmasters. Not the supercomputers.

A pair of amateur players using three ordinary computers.

How?

They weren't the strongest players. Their computers weren't the most powerful. But they were the best at *collaboration*. They knew when to trust the AI, when to override it, and how to synthesize machine calculation with human intuition.

They understood something profound: **the future doesn't belong to humans or machines. It belongs to humans who know how to work with machines.** This is the lesson we've been building toward through every chapter of this book.

AI won't take your job. But it will change it.

The question the only question that matters is this:

Will you lead that change, or be swept along by it?

** ** **

The Mirror Principle

Here's what nobody tells you about AI:

It's a mirror.

It reflects your intentions, your biases, your creativity, and most importantly your choices.

Give AI lazy prompts, you get lazy outputs. Give it thoughtful questions, you get thoughtful responses.

Use it to avoid thinking, you become passive. Use it to enhance thinking, you become sharper.

Outsource your judgment, you become replaceable. Augment your judgment, you become invaluable.

AI doesn't have a will. It has capabilities. What you do with those capabilities is entirely up to you.

This is why two people can use the exact same tool and get radically different results.
One uses ChatGPT to write emails they don't even read before sending.
The other uses it to challenge their ideas, test their arguments, and refine their thinking.

One becomes dependent.
The other becomes dangerous.

The tool is neutral. You are the variable.

** ** **

What We Choose Matters

Let me tell you about two possible futures.

Both are plausible. Both are already happening in different corners of the world.

Which one we get depends on the choices we make individually and collectively in the next few years.

Future A: The Passive Dystopia

In this future, AI becomes so convenient that we stop thinking.

We ask AI to summarize articles, so we stop reading deeply.

We ask AI to solve problems, so we stop developing problem-solving skills.
We ask AI to write, so we stop crafting our own words.

We become *consumers* of AI outputs rather than creators using AI tools.
Work becomes hollow. We're faster, but shallower. More productive, but less creative. More efficient, but less fulfilled.

Companies optimize for speed and scale. Human judgment becomes a bottleneck to eliminate. Workers who "*think too much*" are seen as slow.

Education suffers. Students use AI to write essays without learning to think. They pass tests but don't develop critical reasoning. They graduate with credentials but not competence.

Inequality widens. Those who can afford human mentors, human teachers, human coaches thrive. Everyone else is trained by algorithms that optimize for compliance, not growth.

We save time, but we don't spend it on anything meaningful. We fill the void with more consumption more content, more distraction, more numbing.

We become efficient but empty.

This future isn't far-fetched. We're already seeing early signs.

Future B: The Collaborative Renaissance

In this future, AI liberates us from drudgery so we can focus on what makes us human.

We use AI to handle repetitive tasks, freeing time for creativity, strategy, and connection.

Teachers spend less time grading and more time mentoring.
Doctors spend less time on paperwork and more time with patients.
Designers spend less time on mock-ups and more time on vision.

Work becomes more meaningful. We're not just executing tasks we're solving complex problems, building relationships, creating value that can't be automated.

Education evolves. Students learn *with* AI, not from it. They use AI to explore ideas, test hypotheses, get feedback but they're still doing the thinking. The struggle to learn isn't bypassed; it's supported.

Inequality is addressed. AI democratizes access to expertise. A kid in a rural town can get world-class tutoring. A small business can compete with corporations. Access to knowledge becomes nearly universal.

We reclaim time for what matters: deep work, meaningful relationships, creative pursuits, rest.

We become more capable and more human.

This future is also within reach. We're seeing early signs of it, too.

The difference between these futures isn't the technology. It's how we choose to use it.

Future A happens when we optimize for convenience without thinking about consequences.

Future B happens when we use AI intentionally, with wisdom and balance.

Which future are you building?

** ** **

The Three Principles of Leading AI

If we want Future B the collaborative renaissance we need to operate from three core principles.

Principle 1: AI as Amplifier, Not Replacement

The mindset: AI should make you more of what you are, not less.

If you're creative, AI should help you create more and better.

If you're analytical, AI should help you analyze faster and deeper.
If you're empathetic, AI should free up time for human connection.

The trap to avoid: Using AI to replace the work that develops your skills.

The practice:

- Use AI for tasks you've already mastered
- Do the hard thinking yourself first, then use AI to refine or accelerate
- Regularly work without AI to ensure your core capabilities remain sharp

The test: If AI disappeared tomorrow, could you still do your job well? If yes, you're using it right.

Principle 2: Augment Judgment, Don't Abdicate It

The mindset: AI provides options. You make decisions.

The trap to avoid: Blindly accepting AI's recommendations because they sound authoritative.

The practice:

- Always ask: "*Why is AI suggesting this?*"
- Challenge AI's outputs: "*What are the weaknesses in this approach?*"
- Cross-check critical facts
- Add context AI can't know (your values, your goals, your constraints)

The reminder: AI optimizes for patterns in data. You optimize for meaning, ethics, and long-term consequences.
When the two align, great. When they conflict, you lead.

Principle 3: Stay Curious, Stay Human

The mindset: Technology changes. Humanity doesn't.

The trap to avoid: Letting efficiency eclipse empathy, speed eclipse depth, productivity eclipse purpose.

The practice:

- Protect time for unstructured thinking (walks, journaling, daydreaming)
- Prioritize face-to-face connection over digital efficiency
- Read long-form content, not just summaries
- Practice skills manually, even when AI can do them faster
- Ask "*why*" more than "*how*"

The truth: The most valuable thing you bring to your work isn't your ability to process information. It's your ability to care, to create, to connect, and to choose.

AI can't do that. You can.

** ** **

The Questions We Should Be Asking

As AI becomes more integrated into our lives, we need to ask harder questions not just about productivity, but about meaning.

Here are the questions I think about:

What kind of work is worth doing?

If AI can draft, summarize, analyze, and generate what's left for humans?

The answer: **work that requires us to be fully present.**

- Teaching that adapts to each student's unspoken needs
- Leadership that inspires through vulnerability and vision
- Art that moves people because it's honest and original
- Relationships built on trust and shared experience
- Problems solved through wisdom, not just data

This is the work that AI can't touch. This is the work worth protecting.

What skills should we teach the next generation?
If knowledge is instantly accessible, rote memorization becomes less valuable.

But these skills become *more* valuable:

- Critical thinking (evaluating information, not just consuming it)
- Creativity (generating original ideas, not recombining existing ones)
- Emotional intelligence (reading people, building trust)
- Adaptability (learning how to learn)
- Ethics (making decisions when data alone can't guide you)

We need to shift education from *"what to think"* to *"how to think."*

How do we stay connected in an automated world?

AI can simulate conversation, but it can't replace connection.

As work becomes more automated, we risk becoming more isolated. We text instead of calling. We email instead of meeting. We interact with screens more than people.

The antidote: Deliberately protect human rituals.

- The weekly team lunch
- The in-person brainstorm
- The coffee chat with no agenda
- The handwritten note

These aren't inefficiencies to eliminate. They're what makes work human.

What does success look like in the AI era?

The old definition: Climb the ladder. Maximize income. Accumulate status.

The new definition might be:

- Doing work that matters
- Continuous growth and learning
- Meaningful relationships
- Time for rest and creativity
- Contributing to something larger than yourself

AI can help you achieve all of these if you use it intentionally.

But if you let AI define success for you (optimize engagement, maximize output, hit KPIs), you'll miss the point entirely.

You are not a productivity machine. You're a human being.

The Balance We Need

This entire book has been about balance.

Not "*AI is all good*" or "*AI is all bad.*"

But: **AI is powerful. Use it wisely.**

Here's what balance looks like in practice:
Work

- Use AI to eliminate drudgery, not thinking
- Automate tasks, not relationships
- Increase output, but don't sacrifice depth

Learning

- Use AI as a tutor, not a crutch
- Let AI help you explore, not avoid struggle
- Learn faster, but learn genuinely

Creativity

- Use AI to generate options, not final products
- Let AI inspire, but you create
- Collaborate with AI, but protect your voice

Life

- Use AI to reclaim time, then spend it on what matters
- Don't fill saved time with more work fill it with presence
- Efficiency is a tool, not a goal

** ** **

The Choice Ahead

Let's return to where we started.
Sarah and Michael. Same assignment. Different approaches.

Sarah worked hard. Michael worked smart.

But here's what I didn't tell you: six months later, Sarah learned from Michael.
She started using AI. She got faster. She freed up time.
And she used that time to deepen her expertise, build client relationships, and take on more strategic work.

A year later, both were thriving. Different paths, same destination.

The point isn't that one way is right and one is wrong.

The point is: **adaptability wins.**

Michael adapted early. Sarah adapted later. Both succeeded because they were willing to change.

The only people who lost were those who refused to adapt at all.

** ** **

What I Hope You Take From This Book

If you remember nothing else, remember this:

AI will not take your job. But someone who knows how to use AI will.

And that someone can be you.

You don't need to become a technologist. You don't need to understand neural networks. You just need to be curious, willing to experiment, and committed to staying human.
Use AI to amplify your strengths. Use it to eliminate busy work so you can focus on meaningful work.
Use it to learn faster so you can keep growing.
Use it to work smarter so you have time for what matters.

But never *never* let it replace your judgment, your creativity, your empathy, or your humanity.

You're not competing with AI. You're collaborating with it.

And in that collaboration, the most important variable is you.

** ** **

The Final Exercise: Your AI Manifesto

Before you close this book, take 15 minutes and write your personal AI manifesto.

Answer these questions:

1. **What will I use AI for?**
    (Be specific. Which tasks? Which parts of my work?)
2. **What will I never outsource to AI?**
    (What skills or work are too important to automate?)
3. **How will I protect my humanity?**
    (What practices will keep me sharp, creative, and connected?)
4. **What will I do with the time AI saves me?**
    (More work? Learning? Relationships? Rest?)
5. **How will I measure success?**
    (Not just productivity what actually matters to me?)

Write it down. Keep it somewhere visible.

When you're tempted to let AI do your thinking for you, read it.

When you're wondering if you're using AI right, check it.

This manifesto is your compass. It will keep you on course.

** ** **

The Beginning, Not the End

This book ends here. But your journey with AI is just beginning.

The tools will change. New capabilities will emerge. What's cutting-edge today will be obsolete tomorrow.

But the principles won't change:

- Stay curious
- Keep learning
- Protect your humanity
- Lead the technology, don't follow it

The future isn't something that happens to you. It's something you build, one choice at a time.

And every time you open an AI tool, you're making a choice.

Choose to think, not consume.
Choose to create, not copy.
Choose to lead, not follow.
Choose to become more human, not less.
The machines are getting smarter. Make sure you are, too.

A Final Thought

In 1962, President John F. Kennedy stood at Rice University and declared that America would go to the moon.

"We choose to go to the moon," he said. *"Not because it is easy, but because it is hard."*

He understood something crucial: **challenge is what makes us grow.**

The easy path would've been to let the Soviets win the space race. The hard path was to push human capability to its limits.

They chose the hard path. And it changed history. **You face a similar choice.**

The easy path is to let AI do your thinking, your creating, your problem-solving. To become a passenger in your own career.

The hard path is to use AI as a tool while you stay sharp, stay curious, and stay in command. To become a pilot, not a passenger.

One path leads to convenience and decline. The other leads to growth and resilience.

We choose to use AI wisely not because it is easy, but because it is necessary.

The future is coming whether we're ready or not.

But you? You're going to be ready.

Because you're not waiting for the future. You're building it.

Welcome to the age of human-AI collaboration.

Now go build something remarkable.

RESOURCES FOR CONTINUED LEARNING

AI Tools Mentioned in This Book:

- ChatGPT (OpenAI)
- Claude (Anthropic)
- Gemini (Google)
- Midjourney (Image generation)
- Zapier (Automation)
- Otter.ai (Transcription)

Further Reading:

- *Deep Work* by Cal Newport
- *Atomic Habits* by James Clear
- *The Innovator's Dilemma* by Clayton Christensen
- *Range* by David Epstein
- *Mindset* by Carol Dweck

Online Learning:

- Coursera (AI and machine learning courses)
- Khan Academy (Free courses on emerging tech)
- Fast.ai (Practical AI education)

Communities:

- AI-focused professional groups on LinkedIn
- Industry-specific AI learning communities
- Local meetups and workshops

Stay Updated:

- Follow AI researchers and practitioners on social media
- Subscribe to AI newsletters (The Neuron, AI Breakfast, TLDR AI)
- Set Google Alerts for AI + [your industry]

Remember: The best resource is your own curiosity. Keep experimenting. Keep learning. Keep growing.

THE END

(But really, it's just the beginning.)

ACKNOWLEDGMENTS

This book exists because of many people who believed in it before I did.

To my clients across three continents thank you for trusting me to guide your AI journeys. Your questions, challenges, and successes shaped every framework in these pages. You taught me as much as I taught you.

To the professionals who shared their stories for Chapter 6 your willingness to be vulnerable about your struggles and generous with your lessons made this book real. You are the proof that adaptation works.

To my early readers and beta testers your feedback sharpened every argument, caught every error, and pushed me to clarify what I thought I already understood.

To the researchers, writers, and thought leaders whose work informed this book particularly Cal Newport, James Clear, Yuval Noah Harari, and the teams at OpenAI, Anthropic, and countless research institutions studying AI's impact on work. Your work laid the foundation.

To my family thank you for understanding the late nights, the missed dinners, and my occasional distraction when I was mentally debugging a chapter.

Your support made this possible.

To my mentors and teachers, from engineering school to my first data science role you taught me not just to build with technology, but to think about its impact on humans. That lens shaped everything.

And finally, to you, the reader thank you for caring enough about your future to invest time in this book. The world needs more people like you: curious, adaptable, and committed to growth. Keep learning. Keep adapting. Keep leading.

The future is bright because you're building it.

NOTES AND REFERENCES

A Note on Sources:

The frameworks and advice in this book are drawn from multiple sources: academic research, industry studies, client implementations, and a decade of hands-on experience. I've prioritized accessibility over academic formality, but every major claim is grounded in evidence. Where specific studies or statistics are cited in the text, you'll find the full references below.

The case studies in Chapter 6 are composites based on real patterns observed across multiple clients, with details altered to protect privacy. The strategies, results, and lessons are authentic only the names and identifying details have been changed.

AI tools and capabilities evolve rapidly. Information accurate at publication may change. For updated tool recommendations and resources,
visit **victorleebooks.com**

INTRODUCTION & CHAPTER 1: The Myth of the Job-Stealing Robot

On AI as transformational technology:

- Bezos, Jeff. Interview discussing AI investment and horizontal enabling layer technology. 2024. Referenced for perspective on AI's broad industrial impact and the distinction between technology fundamentals and investment hype.
- Nadella, Satya. Remarks at Microsoft Ignite 2024, Chicago, November 2024. Referenced for perspective on AI as fundamental runtime shaping all applications and platforms.
- Pichai, Sundar. Interview with CBS 60 Minutes, discussing AI as profound technology comparable to fire and electricity. Aired April 17, 2023.

On automation and employment history:

- Autor, David H. "Why Are There Still So Many Jobs? The History and Future of Workplace Automation." *Journal of Economic Perspectives* 29, no. 3 (2015): 3-30. https://doi.org/10.1257/jep.29.3.3
- Frey, Carl Benedikt, and Michael A. Osborne. "The Future of Employment: How Susceptible Are Jobs to Computerisation?" *Technological Forecasting and Social Change* 114 (2017): 254-280.

On the Luddite movement:

- Sale, Kirkpatrick. Rebels Against the Future: *The Luddites and Their War on the Industrial Revolution: Lessons for the Computer Age.* Reading, MA: Addison-Wesley, 1995.

Agricultural employment data:

- U.S. Bureau of Labor Statistics. Historical employment data by industry sector, 1900-2000. Available at bls.gov.

On task automation vs. job automation:

- Acemoglu, Daron, and Pascual Restrepo. "Robots and Jobs: Evidence from US Labor Markets." *Journal of Political Economy* 128, no. 6 (2020): 2188-2244.

CHAPTER 2: Meet Your AI Toolbox

On tool understanding and adoption:

- Altman, Sam. "Technology in a Turbulent World." Session at World Economic Forum, Davos, Switzerland, January 2024. Referenced for perspective on how people naturally understand tool limitations and capabilities.

AI adoption statistics:

- McKinsey Global Institute. "The State of AI in 2023: Generative AI's Breakout Year." McKinsey & Company, August 2023. www.mckinsey.com/capabilities/quantumblack/our-insights

ChatGPT user growth:

- Hu, Krystal. "ChatGPT Sets Record for Fastest-Growing User Base." *Reuters*, February 2, 2023.

CHAPTER 3: The Human Edge

On human-AI collaboration and the value of human connection:

- Altman, Sam. Discussion at World Economic Forum, Davos, January 2024. Referenced for perspective on humans remaining focused on each other despite better tools.
- Nadella, Satya. "The Future of Work with AI." Microsoft keynote address, March 16, 2023. Referenced for perspective on work drudgery versus the soul of work.

AlphaGo vs. Lee Sedol:

- Silver, David, et al. "Mastering the Game of Go with Deep Neural Networks and Tree Search." *Nature* 529, no. 7587 (2016): 484-489. https://doi.org/10.1038/nature16961
- Metz, Cade. "In Two Moves, AlphaGo and Lee Sedol Redefined the Future." *Wired,* March 16, 2016.

Chess popularity post-Deep Blue:

- Chess.com. "2023 Year in Review." Includes user growth statistics and engagement data. www.chess.com/news

Freestyle chess/Advanced chess:

- Kasparov, Garry. "The Chess Master and the Computer." The New York Review of Books, February 11, 2010.
- Kasparov, Garry. *Deep Thinking:* Where Machine Intelligence *Ends and Human Creativity Begins.* New York: PublicAffairs, 2017.

On human-AI collaboration:

- Brynjolfsson, Erik, and Andrew McAfee. The Second Machine Age: *Work, Progress, and Prosperity in a Time of Brilliant Technologies.* New York: W.W. Norton & Company, 2014.

CHAPTER 4: The Lazy Brain Trap

On job transformation and elimination:

- Altman, Sam. Discussion with MIT President Sally Kornbluth, Massachusetts Institute of Technology, May 2, 2024. Referenced for candid perspective on AI's impact on job categories and workforce transformation.

London taxi driver hippocampus studies:

- Maguire, Eleanor A., et al. "Navigation-Related Structural Change in the Hippocampi of Taxi Drivers." *Proceedings of the National Academy of Sciences* 97, no. 8 (2000): 4398-4403. https://doi.org/10.1073/pnas.070039597
- Woollett, Katherine, and Eleanor A. Maguire. "Acquiring 'the Knowledge' of London's Layout Drives Structural Brain Changes." *Current Biology* 21, no. 24 (2011): 2109-2114.

GPS impact on spatial memory and cognition:

- Dahmani, Louisa, and Véronique D. Bohbot. "Habitual Use of GPS Negatively Impacts Spatial Memory During Self-Guided Navigation." *Scientific Reports* 10, no. 1 (2020): 6310. https://doi.org/10.1038/s41598-020-62877-0

The Google Effect/Digital amnesia:

- Sparrow, Betsy, Jenny Liu, and Daniel M. Wegner. "Google Effects on Memory: Cognitive Consequences of Having Information at Our Fingertips." *Science* 333, no. 6043 (2011): 776-778. https://doi.org/10.1126/science.1207745

AI impact on knowledge workers (MIT/Harvard study):

- Dell'Acqua, Fabrizio, et al. "Navigating the Jagged Technological Frontier: Field Experimental Evidence of the Effects of AI on Knowledge Worker Productivity and Quality." Harvard Business School Working Paper No. 24-013, September 2023.

On cognitive offloading:

- Risko, Evan F., and Sam J. Gilbert. "Cognitive Offloading." *Trends in Cognitive Sciences* 20, no. 9 (2016): 676-688.

CHAPTER 5: The Practical Playbook

On experimentation and adoption mindset:

- Nadella, Satya. Remarks at Fast Company Innovation Festival 2024, September 2024. Referenced for advice on technology adoption, experimentation, and changing processes.

Benjamin Bloom's 2 Sigma Problem:

- Bloom, Benjamin S. "The 2 Sigma Problem: The Search for Methods of Group Instruction as Effective as One-to-One Tutoring." *Educational Researcher* 13, no. 6 (1984): 4-16. https://doi.org/10.3102/0013189X013006004

Deliberate practice research:

- Ericsson, K. Anders, Ralf Th. Krampe, and Clemens Tesch-Römer. "The Role of Deliberate Practice in the Acquisition of Expert Performance." *Psychological Review* 100, no. 3 (1993): 363-406.
- Ericsson, K. Anders, and Robert Pool. Peak: *Secrets from the New Science of Expertise.* Boston: Houghton Mifflin Harcourt, 2016.

On effective learning strategies:

- Brown, Peter C., Henry L. Roediger III, and Mark A. McDaniel. *Make It Stick: The Science of Successful Learning.* Cambridge, MA: Belknap Press, 2014.

CHAPTER 6: AI in the Workplace

Note on case studies: The professional stories in Chapter 6 are composites based on patterns observed across multiple real implementations. Names, industries, and specific details have been altered to protect client confidentiality, but the strategies, frameworks, and outcomes represent actual results from AI adoption projects.

Supporting research on AI in professional work:

- McKinsey Global Institute. "The Economic Potential of Generative AI: The Next Productivity Frontier." June 2023.
- MIT Sloan Management Review and BCG. "Expanding AI's Impact with Organizational Learning." Research Report, 2022.

CHAPTER 7: Lifelong Learning in the AI Era

On the evolution of work and abstraction levels:
- Altman, Sam. "Technology in a Turbulent World." World Economic Forum, Davos, January 2024. Referenced for vision of how work will operate at higher levels of abstraction with AI assistance.

Keynes's prediction:
- Keynes, John Maynard. "Economic Possibilities for Our Grandchildren" (1930). In *Essays in Persuasion*, 358-373. New York: W.W. Norton & Co., 1963.

Skill half-life research:

* IBM Institute for Business Value. "The Enterprise Guide to Closing the Skills Gap: Strategies for Building and Maintaining a Skilled Workforce." IBM Corporation, 2019.
* Deming, David J., and Lisa B. Kahn. "Skill Requirements Across Firms and Labor Markets: Evidence from Job Postings for Professionals." *Journal of Labor Economics* 36, no. S1 (2018): S337-S369.

Medical knowledge doubling time:

* Densen, Peter. "Challenges and Opportunities Facing Medical Education." *Transactions of the American Clinical and Climatological Association* 122 (2011): 48-58.

On growth mindset:

* Dweck, Carol S. Mindset: *The New Psychology of Success.* New York: Random House, 2006.

On learning transfer and generalization:

* Barnett, Susan M., and Stephen J. Ceci. "When and Where Do We Apply What We Learn? A Taxonomy for Far Transfer." *Psychological Bulletin* 128, no. 4 (2002): 612-637.

CHAPTER 8: A Balanced Future

On AI unlocking human creative potential:

- Pichai, Sundar. "AI Action Summit Remarks." Paris, France, February 10, 2025. Referenced for vision of AI freeing humans from mundane tasks to focus on creative potential.
- Pichai, Sundar. "The AI Platform Shift and the Opportunity Ahead." Carnegie Mellon University President's Lecture Series, September 18, 2024.

On human-AI collaboration:

- Daugherty, Paul R., and H. James Wilson. *Human + Machine: Reimagining Work in the Age of AI.* Boston: Harvard Business Review Press, 2018.

On technology and human values:

- Winner, Langdon. "Do Artifacts Have Politics?" *Daedalus* 109, no. 1 (1980): 121-136.
- Vallor, Shannon. *Technology and the Virtues: A Philosophical Guide to a Future Worth Wanting.* New York: Oxford University Press, 2016.

GENERAL REFERENCES

Books on AI and the future of work:

- Ford, Martin. Rise of the Robots: *Technology and the Threat of a Jobless Future.* New York: Basic Books, 2015.
- Harari, Yuval Noah. *21 Lessons for the 21st Century.* New York: Spiegel & Grau, 2018.
- Schwab, Klaus. *The Fourth Industrial Revolution.* New York: Currency, 2017.
- Susskind, Richard, and Daniel Susskind. *The Future of the Professions: How Technology Will Transform the Work of Human Experts.* Oxford: Oxford University Press, 2015.

Books on learning and skill development:

- Clear, James. *Atomic Habits:* An Easy & Proven Way to Build Good Habits & Break Bad Ones. New York: Avery, 2018.
- Epstein, David. Range: *Why Generalists Triumph in a Specialized World.* New York: Riverhead Books, 2019.
- Newport, Cal. *Deep Work: Rules for Focused Success in a Distracted World.* New York: Grand Central Publishing, 2016.
- Newport, Cal. *So Good They Can't Ignore You: Why Skills Trump Passion in the Quest for Work You Love.* New York: Grand Central Publishing, 2012.

On human cognition and technology:

- Carr, Nicholas. *The Shallows: What the Internet Is Doing to Our Brains.* New York: W.W. Norton & Company, 2010.
- Kahneman, Daniel. *Thinking, Fast and Slow.* New York: Farrar, Straus and Giroux, 2011.

Research institutions and ongoing resources:

- Stanford Human-Centered AI Institute (HAI): hai.stanford.edu
- MIT Work of the Future Initiative: workofthefuture.mit.edu
- OpenAI Research: openai.com/research
- Anthropic Safety Research: anthropic.com/research

RECOMMENDED RESOURCES

For readers who want to go deeper, here are curated resources organized by topic:

Getting Started with AI Tools

Conversational AI:

- ChatGPT (OpenAI): chat.openai.com
- Claude (Anthropic): claude.ai
- Gemini (Google): gemini.google.com

AI for Specific Tasks:

- Grammarly (writing assistant): grammarly.com
- Otter.ai (transcription): otter.ai
- Midjourney (image generation): midjourney.com
- GitHub Copilot (code assistance): github.com/features/copilot

Automation Platforms:

- Zapier: zapier.com
- Make.com: make.com

Learning Resources

Online Courses:

- "AI For Everyone" by Andrew Ng (Coursera)
- "Introduction to Artificial Intelligence" (edX)
- Fast.ai courses (practical AI): fast.ai
- Khan Academy AI courses (free): khanacademy.org

YouTube Channels:

- Two Minute Papers (AI research explained)
- Lex Fridman (AI interviews and discussions)
- 3Blue1Brown (mathematical concepts behind AI)

Newsletters:

- The Neuron (AI news): theneurondaily.com
- TLDR AI (tech summary): tldr.tech/ai
- AI Breakfast (daily digest): aibreakfast.beehiiv.com

BOOKS FOR CONTINUED READING

On AI and Technology:

- *Co-Intelligence: Living and Working with AI* by Ethan Mollick
- *The Alignment Problem* by Brian Christian
- *Life 3.0* by Max Tegmark

On Learning and Growth:

- *Ultralearning* by Scott Young
- *The First 20 Hours* by Josh Kaufman
- *Peak* by Anders Ericsson

On the Future of Work:

- *The Future of the Professions* by Richard and Daniel Susskind
- *Humans Are Underrated* by Geoff Colvin
- *The Inevitable* by Kevin Kelly

COMMUNITIES AND FORUMS

Online Communities:

- r/artificial (Reddit)
- r/ChatGPT (Reddit)
- AI Discord servers (search for topic-specific)
- LinkedIn AI groups

Professional Organizations:

- Association for the Advancement of Artificial Intelligence (AAAI)
- Society for Human Resource Management (SHRM) - AI initiatives
- Association for Talent Development (ATD)

Tools for Tracking AI Developments

- Google Alerts: Set alerts for "AI + [your industry]"
- Feedly: RSS reader for tech news
- Papers with Code: Research papers with implementations
- Hugging Face: AI model repository and community

CORPORATE RESOURCES

If you're implementing AI in your organization:

- Microsoft AI Business School: microsoft.com/ai/ai-business-school
- Google Cloud AI Training: cloud.google.com/training/machinelearning-ai
- AWS Machine Learning University: aws.amazon.com/machine-learning/mlu

VICTOR LEE'S RESOURCES

For ongoing support and updates:

- Website: victorlee.ai
- Newsletter: "The AI Advantage" (weekly insights)
- Free AI Readiness Assessment
- Workshop and speaking inquiries: speaking@victorleebooks.com

Downloadable materials:

- Quick Start Guide (PDF)
- Chapter worksheets
- Prompt library
- 30-day learning challenge tracker

DISCUSSION GUIDE FOR BOOK CLUBS AND TEAMS

This guide is designed for book clubs, reading groups, corporate teams, and classrooms using Adapt or Automate as a discussion text.

How to Use This Guide

For Book Clubs:

- Select 2-3 questions per chapter for 60-90 minute discussions
- Encourage members to share personal experiences
- Focus on practical application, not just theory

For Corporate Teams:

- Use as basis for workshop sessions
- Have team members complete exercises before meetings
- Identify collective actions to implement frameworks
- Track progress over 8-week implementation period

For Classrooms:

- Assign chapters with corresponding exercises
- Use questions for written reflections or group discussions
- Invite students to present their AI experiments
- Final project: Personal AI Manifesto presentation

INTRODUCTION & CHAPTER 1 Questions

1. Before reading this book, what was your gut reaction when you heard "AI is coming for jobs"? Has your perspective shifted?
2. Sarah vs. Michael which one were you more like before reading? Which one do you want to be?
3. The author argues "tasks disappear, jobs evolve." Can you think of examples from your industry where this has already happened?
4. What's your biggest fear about AI in your specific role? After Chapter 1, does that fear feel more or less manageable?
5. Exercise debrief: What did your Reality Check reveal about where you currently stand?

CHAPTER 2 Questions

1. Of the four core AI tools (conversational AI, automation, transcription, image generation), which would be most immediately useful in your work?
2. The "calculator analogy" do you agree that AI is like calculators for knowledge work? Why or why not?
3. What limitations of AI surprised you most? How does knowing these limitations change how you'll use AI?
4. Have you tried any AI tools since reading this chapter? What was your experience?
5. Exercise debrief: Share what happened when you tried your first AI task.

CHAPTER 3 Questions

1. Which of the five human skills (empathy, judgment, creativity, cross-domain synthesis, relationships) is your strongest? Your weakest?
2. Do the two-column exercise together: What percentage of your work is "Column A" (AI could do) vs. "Column B" (requires humanity)?
3. The author claims "soft skills are now hard currency." Do you see evidence of this in your workplace?
4. Think of someone in your field who's truly irreplaceable. What makes them so? How much of that is "human edge"?
5. Exercise debrief: What did you discover about your irreplaceable work?

CHAPTER 4 Questions

1. Have you noticed cognitive decline from over-relying on technology (GPS, autocorrect, search engines)? Share examples.
2. Rate yourself honestly: Are you more "pilot" or "passenger" when using technology?
3. Which of the four cognitive traps resonates most with you personally?
   - Accuracy Illusion
   - Depth Sacrifice
   - Creativity Shortcut
   - Skill Erosion

4. The Blackout Test: If AI disappeared tomorrow, how confident are you in your core skills?
5. Exercise debrief: What did your Dependency Audit reveal?

CHAPTER 5 Questions

1. Try the prompt evolution together: Take a vague prompt and improve it using the frameworks from this chapter.
2. The 6-step learning loop which step do most people skip? Which step do YOU skip?
3. Choose a profession from the examples (teacher, lawyer, entrepreneur, designer, manager). What surprised you about how they use AI?
4. What's one thing you could start learning TODAY using AI as a tutor?
5. Exercise debrief: Share progress on your First Learning Project.

CHAPTER 6 Questions

1. Which success story (Rachel, Marcus, Kira, David, Alicia, Terrance) resonated most with you? Why?
2. What patterns did you notice across all six stories?
3. What mistake did Kira make (the Instagram caption fail)? Have you made similar mistakes?
4. If you could interview one of these six people, what would you ask them?
5. Exercise debrief: What's YOUR transformation moment going to be?

CHAPTER 7 Questions

1. Are you more like Jamie (static professional) or Jordan (adaptive professional) currently?
2. What skills do you have that are "decaying" becoming less valuable over time?
3. Of the five components in the Continuous Learning System, which will be hardest for you to implement?
   ◦ Curiosity Budget
   ◦ Learning Sprint
   ◦ Signal Detection
   ◦ Deliberate Practice
   ◦ Knowledge Capture

4. Which mindset shift do you need most?
   ◦ "I don't know" → "I don't know yet"
   ◦ Expertise → Curiosity
   ◦ Perfectionism → Iteration
   ◦ Scarcity → Abundance
   ◦ Comfort → Challenge

5. Exercise debrief: Share your learning system plans.

CHAPTER 8 Questions

1. Which future seems more likely right now: Future A (Passive Dystopia) or Future B (Collaborative Renaissance)?
2. Of the Three Principles of Leading AI, which will you struggle with most?
   - AI as Amplifier, Not Replacement
   - Augment Judgment, Don't Abdicate It
   - Stay Curious, Stay Human
3. What does "success" look like for you in the AI era? Has your definition changed after reading this book?
4. If you could add one chapter to this book, what would it be about?
5. Exercise debrief: Share your AI Manifesto. What principles will guide

ABOUT THE AUTHOR

Victor Lee is a data scientist, AI strategist, and sought-after advisor to organizations navigating the intelligent automation revolution.

With a background in engineering and advanced training in data science, Victor has spent over a decade at the intersection of technology and business transformation. He's worked as a data analyst and AI implementation specialist for both public institutions and private enterprises across three continents, from startups to Fortune 500 companies.

What sets Victor apart isn't just his technical expertise it's his track record of translating AI capabilities into tangible business outcomes. He's helped small businesses double their revenue through intelligent process automation, guided multinational corporations through digital transformation initiatives, and advised government agencies on data-driven policy decisions. His clients span healthcare, finance, retail, manufacturing, and technology sectors.

Victor's approach is refreshingly practical: he doesn't believe in AI for AI's sake. Instead, he focuses on the human side of technological change helping professionals understand not just *how* AI works, but *how to work with AI* in ways that enhance rather than diminish human capability.

A frequent speaker on AI adoption and workforce transformation, Victor has delivered workshops and keynotes across multiple countries, always emphasizing the same core message: **adaptation beats automation, and humans who learn to collaborate with AI will outperform both humans who resist it and machines working alone.**

Adapt or Automate represents the culmination of Victor's years helping professionals navigate technological disruption. It's the book he wishes he could have given to every client, colleague, and conference attendee who asked him: "What should I actually *do* about AI?"

Victor currently divides his time between consulting work, speaking engagements, and helping organizations build AI-ready cultures. When he's not evangelizing human-AI collaboration, he's experimenting with emerging AI tools, studying the latest research on learning and adaptation, and mentoring the next generation of data professionals.

Connect with Victor:
Website: victorleebooks.com
LinkedIn: /in/victorleebooks
Twitter/X: @victorleebooks
Email: hello@victorleebooks.com

For speaking engagements, corporate workshops, or consulting inquiries: speaking@victorleebooks.com